The
Pastor-Evangelist

Preacher, Model, and Mobilizer
for Church Growth

Edited by
Roger S. Greenway

Presbyterian and Reformed Publishing Company
Phillipsburg, New Jersey

"Preaching and Evangelism" was first published in the *Reformed Ecumenical Synod Mission Bulletin* 4, 2 (February, 1984).

Unless otherwise indicated, Scripture quotations are from the New International Version.

Printed in the United States of America

Library of Congress Cataloging-in-Publication Data

The Pastor-evangelist : preacher, model, and
  mobilizer for church growth.

  Includes bibliographies.
  1. Clergy—Office.   2. Evangelistic work.
3. Church growth.   I. Greenway, Roger S.
BV660.2.P265   1986   253   86-22629
ISBN 0-87552-279-3 (pbk.)

Contents

Foreword

This book is based on Paul's exhortation to Timothy in II Timothy 4:5: "Do the work of an evangelist, discharge all the duties of your ministry." Our purpose is to explore and develop the implications of the biblical mandate for pastors, missionaries, and persons in training for these offices around the world. The book is aimed at the revitalization of churches through pastoral leaders who effectively fulfill their responsibilities to both the faithful sheep in the congregations and the lost and straying outside. By examining scriptural principles and contemporary paradigms of pastoral evangelism, readers may deepen their understanding and widen their vision of pastoral ministry. Churches and leaders in the Reformed and Presbyterian tradition are the primary focus, though the discussions on every page have universal application.

The need for this book stems from several factors. First, the world needs to be evangelized, and the church is God's chief agent. It is "through the church" that God in this age chooses to declare His redemptive purpose in Christ to the world (Eph. 3:10). Yet many churches are ineffective in evangelism, pastors are uncertain of their roles, seminarians worry that they lack evangelistic skills, and churches are sometimes obstacles to rather than instruments of evangelism. As a result all kinds of para-church mission agencies spring up as God's people look elsewhere for leadership in evangelism.

Second, there is a growing awareness in many denominations of the importance of evangelism and the relation between evangelism and church renewal. Part of the evangelical awakening that is occurring today translates into increased pressure on pastors to lead their congregations to growth and outreach. Many pastors are not prepared for this. They feel threatened and embarrassed by the subject of evangelism, and the excellent church growth literature that is available does not quite meet them where they are.

Third and foremost, the Scriptures demand that we take a fresh look at what God requires of pastors. Are there dimensions to pastoring that we have ignored or are pressed into neglecting? An earlier writer on this subject, Charles L. Goodell, expressed the challenge this way: "'Fulfill thy ministry', said the apostle to his son in the Gospel. Many things enter into the pastor's ministry. He must be a student, he must be a preacher, he must be a teacher and a citizen, but everything that he does is of value only as it makes possible the one thing for which he is in the ministry. Even preaching, which is doubtless the highest function of the ministry, is only a means to an end. If the great end is not accomplished, how futile becomes the means!"[1]

Now is the hour for the principles and methods of pastoral evangelism to be re-examined from the Scriptures and from the practical experience of people immersed in church ministry, for a fresh and exciting spirit is sweeping many branches of Christ's church. After many years in which evangelism was relegated to a small group of enthusiasts, church leaders are taking a fresh look at their assignment to advance Christ's kingdom through evangelism and at the causes of the church's ineffectiveness and decline. Furthermore, Christian laymen around the world are looking for pastors who can lead them to growth and renewal.

The writers of these chapters are committed to the church, to evangelism, and to pastoring in the full biblical sense. They are not mere theoreticians, but people with years of practical experience in Christian ministry. They write of what they know and practice. Doctrinally and ecclesiastically they represent the Reformed and Presbyterian tradition. Their desire is to see churches in this and

---

1. Charles L. Goodell, *Pastor and Evangelist* (New York: George H. Doran, 1922), p. vii.

other traditions glow afresh with evangelistic power and fervor. Their concern for seminarians as future church leaders and for more effective ways of preparing people for pastoral ministry is demonstrated by the work they did in preparing this publication after first presenting the material to students at Westminster Theological Seminary in Philadelphia.

This book is intended for pastors, missionaries, and seminarians in this country and around the world. My own experience, first as a pastor and missionary, and second as a teacher of missions, has made me keenly aware of both the exhilarations and the frustrations of pastoral and missionary ministry. When I began my ministry as a missionary-pastor in Asia, I did not know how to pastor and evangelize effectively at the same time. As years passed, I saw the difficulties hampering fellow pastors and missionaries because they did not know how to blend caring for God's people with outreach to the unsaved and unchurched. In the literature on pastoral ministry I see sharp theoretical lines drawn between pastoral care and evangelism, and I realize it is mistaken and damaging to the church. But I also see the beautiful churches and fruitful ministries of those who successfully unite faithfulness to God's Word and people with missionary outreach. And I yearn to see this reproduced in the ministries of the people being trained in Christian colleges and seminaries.

Perhaps, from history's viewpoint, this will be the area in which American theology will make its greatest contribution. Growth through missions and evangelism has been a characteristic mark of Christianity in this country from the start, and something of the spirit of Jonathan Edwards, the great New England Calvinist pastor of the eighteenth century, is reflected in this book. Edwards was many things: man of deep personal piety, churchman, keen theologian, gifted writer and preacher. His work laid the foundation for the Great Awakening and the missionary movement that followed it. In everything Edwards was an evangelist, dedicated to missionary-minded Calvinism and the kind of churches that would be transforming influences in society. His commitment to social justice as well as to evangelism was shown by his fiery defense of the Housatonics against white exploiters during his time of mission work among the Indians in Stockbridge, Massachusetts. Like Edwards in his generation, we today must strive to be faithful to our calling as church leaders, pastor-evangelists, defenders of truth and righteousness. The pursuance of such ministry is the goal of this book.

Roger S. Greenway
Editor

— 1 —

Jesus, the Pastor-Evangelist
Roger S. Greenway

Twenty years ago, my friend and missionary colleague Richard De Ridder was eating breakfast in his home in Colombo, Sri Lanka, when the telephone rang. On the line was the pastor of one of the larger churches in Colombo, a man in his mid-fifties. He had pastored for three decades and occupied a position of influence and leadership in the church community. But his voice that morning sounded troubled. "Richard," he said, "there's a Buddhist monk at my door who says he wants to become a Christian. What do I do with him?"

Richard De Ridder tactfully suggested that the two men sit down and examine verses in the Bible that explain the gospel and God's provision of salvation through faith in Christ. "But Richard," said the pastor, "I'm not good at that kind of thing. Can you come over here and deal with him?"

As quickly as he could, Richard De Ridder got into his car and drove to the manse. There on the verandah sat the clergyman of another religion dressed in his colorful robes. His story was long and fascinating. He had studied the Bible for several years. He had taken correspondence courses and read Christian literature sent him by mail. Finally he made up his mind to become a Christian. He knew nothing about different churches and denominations, so he picked out the biggest church on Galle Road and went to see the clergyman in charge. De Ridder spent the rest of the day with him, answering questions and explaining the essentials of the Christian

1

faith. By nightfall the man was asking how soon he could be baptized.

The incident on the verandah of the Colombo manse illustrates a missing link in pastoral ministry—the evangelistic dimension. The pastor who did not know what to do with the priest was a leader in his church and denomination. He had pastored a large congregation for many years. But when the opportunity arose that might have been a high point in his ministry, he turned it over to someone else because he simply did not know how to evangelize. As a pastor he had many skills, but in one key area of ministry he was seriously deficient. His church reflected it, for like the pastor, the church had many assets, but in evangelism and outreach to the Buddhist community it hardly did anything.

Observations I have made over three decades of ministry in the United States, Latin America, and Asia have convinced me that the separation in theory and practice between pastoral work and evangelism is one of the chief sources of the church's weakness and explains why many churches do not grow. This flaw is not restricted to any one denomination or theological tradition, though mainline churches seem particularly vulnerable; nor is the problem limited to Western countries, where there are many old churches. Churches in the developing nations suffer from the malady also.

Over against this, my study of the Scriptures has convinced me that the evangelistic dimension is so inherent in the pastoral office that to neglect it is rank disobedience to God. The Bible makes evangelism not a pastoral option, but a pastoral mandate. We will now examine some of the key Scripture passages that deal with this subject.

Ezekiel 34 and Shepherds That Failed

Ezekiel 34 describes the shepherds (pastors) of ancient Israel who were concerned about themselves but failed to care for the sheep. The Lord's assessment of their ministry is expressed as follows:

> The Word of the Lord came to me: "Son of man, prophesy against the shepherds of Israel; prophesy and say to them: 'This

is what the Sovereign Lord says: Woe to the shepherds of Israel who only take care of themselves! Should not the shepherds take care of the flock?'" (vv. 1-2).

The Lord holds the slothful shepherds fully accountable for their poor performance and declares that He intends to remove them from tending the flock. He will replace them with a true shepherd, a shepherd who will express the heart of God toward the flock by the way he cares for them.

Notice the precise ways these ancient shepherds failed. "You have not strengthened the weak or healed the sick or bound up the injured. You have not brought back the strays or searched for the lost. . . . They were scattered over the whole earth, and no one searched or looked for them" (vv. 4-6). Israel's leaders did not do what they were called and appointed to do. They fed themselves through their offices, but let people go spiritually hungry. The shepherds served insofar as it was convenient, but healing, searching, finding the lost was too hard work. People strayed and were not followed. They were lost, and Israel's leaders paid no attention. Finally, the Lord said He would replace the slothful leaders, and He Himself would search for the sheep and look after them. As a shepherd looks after his scattered flock, so the Lord would look after His sheep. He would rescue them from all the places where they were snared. Not sparing Himself, He would save them.

Jesus Christ is the faithful Shepherd who fulfills the ministry that Israel's leaders forsook. Christ is the one whom Ezekiel foresees across the coming ages, and by his prophecy Ezekiel comforts God's people: "For this is what the Sovereign Lord says: I myself will search for my sheep and look after them. As a shepherd looks after his scattered flock when he is with them, so will I look after my sheep. I will rescue them from all the places where they were scattered" (vv. 11-12).

Jesus, the Perfect Model

In the light of Ezekiel's warning and God's promise to send a faithful shepherd, Jesus' words in John 10 have particular import: "I am the good shepherd. The good shepherd lays down his life for the sheep" (v. 11). Jesus is the perfect pastor-shepherd. He sacrifices Himself for the good of the sheep. He does perfectly what the ancient leaders of Israel failed to do. He feeds, heals, seeks, and finds the hungry, lost, and dying members of the fold. Jesus says moreover, "Other sheep I have that are not of this fold [old Israel], they too will hear my call, and they shall become one flock with one shepherd" (v. 16).

Jesus, the perfect model of the godly pastor, blends care for the faithful with pursuit of the lost. By direct discourse, personal example, and parables Jesus teaches the nature and functions of New Testament pastoring. Teaching, He feeds. Itinerating, He seeks the scattered ones. Sending the disciples, He widens the scope of ministry to the farthest corners. He announces to the lost and dying that God's true Shepherd has come, and there is room in His sheep pen for them. Jesus defends those whom He has gathered against malicious attackers so that none can snatch them out of His hand (John 10:7). In every way Jesus demonstrates the godly heart of the pastor who at great sacrifice to himself, even unto death, comes to seek and to save the lost.

In the parable of the lost sheep (Matt. 18:12-14; Luke 15:4-7), Jesus describes His joy and the Father's when He finds lost sheep after a long and arduous search. It is greater than His joy over the ninety-nine who stayed on the right path. This is the "soteriological joy of God" by which Jesus defends His love for sinners against the criticism of His opponents. The pastoral heart of God is revealed in the home-bound shepherd carrying the sheep in his arms. God, like the happy shepherd, is filled with boundless joy at the bringing back of the lost. *The fetching of sinners home is the saving office of Pastor Jesus, the shepherd of prophecy, true Messiah, perfect model for all who follow His ministry.* Those who ignore His example also refuse His heart and place themselves in the company of Pharisees and the despised shepherds of Ezekiel's book. In essence they reject the cross, where the divine Shepherd made atoning sacrifice for lost and rebellious sheep.

No other religion in all human history teaches about a shepherd like this. Nor is there anything like the pastoral office in other faiths. Jesus has stamped it with a decisive mark, the readiness to give one's life for the flock and a self-sacrificing passion that lost ones be saved.

The Bible calls Jesus the "Chief Shepherd" (I Pet. 5:4) under whom all the church's under-shepherds—pastors and missionaries—serve and in whom they find their model and inspiration. He is also the "great Shepherd" (Heb. 13:20) to whom all must answer as to their resemblance to Him in heart, attitude, and ministry. His office as Shepherd is not restricted to national Israel, for there are "other sheep" (John 10:6) included in His life-giving sacrifice, and He is intent on bringing them into the fold.

All mission work and evangelism spring from this intent, the redemptive purpose of the Savior-Shepherd to fill His sheep pen with all for whom He died. Pastors and missionaries together serve that purpose. They proclaim the one gospel under the same commission (Matt. 28:19). In Christ their work is one.

Paradigms of Pastoral Evangelism in Acts

In Acts, the Jesus model is worked out in the ministries of the apostles. There we find the paradigms from which all who bear office take their cue. The disciples were taught and trained by Jesus for the apostolate to which He later commissioned them. They were further led by the Holy Spirit in such a manner that their ministries as well as their words remain models for the church in all ages. Peter and Paul, about whom we know most, moved back and forth between discipling believers and evangelizing the lost.

Peter, who was exhorted by the risen Lord to "pastor my little sheep" (John 21:16), is later pulled by the Spirit to do cross-cultural evangelism in the house of Cornelius (Acts 10). Already in Acts 9:32-43, we see Peter itinerating and evangelizing, along with healing Aeneas, the paralyzed man, and raising Dorcas back to life. Peter's activities are reminiscent of the itinerating-healing-preaching ministry of Jesus. Could we expect anything different?

Paul's ministry blended evangelism, pastoral care, church organization, and theological instruction. In Acts 20:17-38, Paul lays before the elders of the church at Ephesus the course of his ministry among them as an example for them to follow. He had blended ministry to Jews and to Greeks, public testimony, and house-to-house visitation. Insulted and harassed by opponents, he had struggled to win converts, disciple the believers, and organize the church with its leadership. In other words, Paul was a missionary, a pastor, a defender of the faith, a theologian and teacher, and a church planter. He was also the inspired writer of Scripture through whose entire ministry of preaching, writing, and other labors the spirit of evangelism breathed.

Timothy's Task as Defined by Paul

In the light of what we have seen it comes as no surprise that Timothy's task as defined by Paul in II Timothy 4:5 includes the admonition to "do the work of an evangelist, discharge all the duties of your ministry." The work of vangelism is *hard* work (*ergou*). The evangelist's task has always been arduous, often frustrating, and the timid or halfhearted might easily abandon it. Good men can burn out, and in Acts at least one did (John Mark, Acts 13:13). Timothy, it appears, was not an aggressive individual and tended toward reticence in public testimony. In his second letter to Timothy, Paul says explicitly, "God did not give us a spirit of timidity, but a spirit of power, of love and self-discipline. So do not be ashamed to testify about our Lord . . . but join with me in suffering for the gospel, by the power of God (II Tim. 1:7-8). In view of Timothy's timidity and the stiff opposition from gospel deniers, Paul realized that Timothy needed explicit encouragement to persist in evangelism.

Precisely what was Paul instructing Timothy to do? Was he burdening Timothy with a second ministry, in addition to that of pastoring and organizing the young church? Did Timothy have two jobs, that of pastor *and* evangelist? Not at all. William Hendriksen, in his *New Testament Commentary* on I and II Timothy, points out that in Greek the word translated *evangelist* is not preceded by the definite article. This suggests that it was not Paul's intention to assign Timothy a second job, but instead to stress the evangelistic character, the quality and nature, of all his pastoral duties. When Paul adds, "do the work of an evangelist," he is saying, *Timothy, your pastoral work should be evangelistic in character throughout.* You are never a pastor without being an evangelist.

In other words, Timothy is to be a bringer of good news in every situation, in the pulpit or on the street. Evangelism is not a "second hat" he sometimes wears, but it is woven into the entire fabric of the one hat he is to wear all the time.

The pastor-evangelist is always looking out for lost souls. He keeps an eye open for straying sheep night and day. He goes out of his way to look for them and to guide them back to the Lord wherever he finds them. He sees to it that there is an evangelistic tone to all his teaching and preaching. He knows that there are children who have not committed their hearts to God. He knows that in every audience there may be unsaved though professing church members. And often there are nonmembers listening in. The pastor-evangelist keeps all of these in mind, and he is particularly solicitous of those whose minds and hearts have been bruised and tormented by sin. Sometimes he has to turn a deaf ear for a while to the clamor of the sheep pen in order to go out looking for the lost and bring them home.

Paul is not suggesting that a pastor should forsake his congregation in order to go from place to place for extended periods holding evangelistic meetings and planting churches. Itinerating evangelism and church planting, according to Ephesians 4:11, belong to a special class of men especially gifted and appointed for that work. But II Timothy 4:5 means that the local pastor should be evangelistic in his message and methods. In the regular course of his preaching, teaching, visiting, counseling, leading, and organizing, he should reach out to the lost with the intent of bringing them to Christ and the church. Then he will be discharging faithfully and fully the duties of his ministry. Motivated and instructed by their pastor's word and example, church members will likewise live, serve, and speak in ways that call lost ones home.

Through the application of that principle, the apostolate continues. Immediately following his clear injunction to Timothy, the apostle speaks of his own departure from the scene (II Tim. 4:6ff.). The apostolate must go on, however, though not in the narrow sense of the direct ministries of Jesus' first disciples, who were inspired by the Holy Spirit to write His Word and lay the foundations of the New Testament church. But the mission, the work to which the founders were committed, must continue after Paul and the others have died. "God buries the workers, but the work goes on." It continues wherever caring for the sheep and seeking the lost go together. So Timothy the pastor-organizer must also be Timothy the evangelist, establishing a paradigm for those who succeed him.

In summary, the pastor's task is to care for the congregation (Acts 20:28; I Pet. 5:2-4), seek the lost (Matt. 18:12-14; Luke 11:23), and defend believers from heresy (Acts 20:29ff.). The pastor's fulfillment of this task will be an example for the flock to follow (I Pet. 5:3). At His appearing the Chief Pastor will honor those who have discharged their ministry faithfully (I Pet. 5:4). Together with elders, pastors should reflect often on this New Testament description of church ministry, for it is their divine mandate as "shepherds of the church" (Acts 20:28).

Applying This Teaching Today

Strong and growing churches are churches that enjoy the kind of pastoral leadership portrayed in the New Testament. Pastors differ in respect to gifts and personalities, and leaders in the early church did too. But they understand their mandate and the roles that accompany it, and they are committed to discharging all its duties. Coupled with trust in the Holy Spirit to empower God's servants for the work given them, this personal acceptance of the wide range of demands that accompany church leadership is fundamental for young pastors and those whose ministries need renewing.

Show me any place in the world where the gospel is moving forward and churches are growing, and I will show you Christian leadership that reflects this teaching. By the same token, show me stagnant churches, concerned only with internal matters, and I will have no difficulty pointing out breakdowns in pastoral leadership, lack of courage, and failure to discharge the evangelistic dimensions of the pastoral office in the public arena.

It takes time before the average congregation develops enough concern for outreach that it is willing to be neglected in order that the lost and unchurched be served and saved. I mention this because it is the universal experience of pastors that congregations tend to monopolize the pastor's time. In the minds of some members, the pastor never does enough for them. Therefore he must patiently and persistently teach first the elders and then the entire membership that his calling, and theirs, includes outreach to the community at large. This is an educational process, and it is very important for the pastor's ministry. There are occasions when pastors must make hard decisions, with no time to discuss the issues or prepare people to understand. The perception of ministry that the pastor has built up in the congregation over the course of time will serve him well in times of critical decision.

An illustration of this comes from the experience of a young pastor in a small midwestern town. He received two phone calls, one right after the other. Two men were dying, one was being rushed at that moment to a hospital to the west of town and the other was already admitted to a hospital thirty minutes to the east. Both men were calling for the pastor. One was an elder in the church, and the other was a God-denying individual, well known in the community for his dislike of the church and everything it stood for. In their moment of crisis, both were calling for God's servant, but the two hospitals were in opposite directions. The pastor had to decide which to visit first.

He prayed, and then hurried to the bedside of the dying unsaved sinner. He reasoned that the elder was saved but the other man was not. He made his choice based on his concept of ministry and the soteriological priorities he believed. As it turned out, the tough old sinner repented. Before he died he put his faith in Jesus and died in peace. The elder, on the other hand, recovered and left the church. He and his relatives were furious because the pastor had not come immediately to his hospital room. The pastor's decision became an issue for the whole church, and members talked about it for months. The pastor's action at that critical moment became an object lesson that none of them missed.

A pastor cannot expect to gain the support of every member in the congregation, but he certainly must work to gain the support and understanding of the elders and deacons. They must come to see that the pastor has a duty to the unsaved as well as to the regular members and back him when issues arise. Neglect for evangelism's sake is not the type of neglect that causes churches to suffer. It is not laziness, for evangelistic efforts usually cost the pastor dearly in terms of strain on himself, longer hours, and tough choices. But with God's blessing and prayer such efforts mean the salvation of the lost and the enrichment of the church.

Consciously or unconsciously, every congregation tends to monopolize every ounce of the pastor's time and energy, and for that reason pastors periodically need to reassess their activities. One question they must face is whether they are neglecting some important aspects of their ministry. Are they maintaining a biblical balance? In doing this they must not pay too much attention to the whispering of certain members who immediately conclude they are cheated if the pastor spends time with nonmembers.

I recall a certain day in my pastoral ministry when the Lord sent me an unusual number of opportunities to witness for Christ outside the congregation. Unsaved and unchurched people, particularly because of the good work of our deacons, had come to me for prayer and counsel. Toward the end of a busy afternoon of appointments and phone calls, I received a call from one of the local hospitals that a man was dying who had no church or pastor and his wife had asked that I come immediately. A certain member stood in the church office as I put on my coat and explained to the church secretary where I was going. As I left the room the member murmured half under his breath but loud enough for me to hear, "It looks like our pastor spends most of his day on people who don't attend this church."

Ouch! I felt the barb in that remark. The member might just as well have added what was in his mind, "And they are people who don't pay your salary." I knew him and his coolness toward outreach very well, and I admit that as I got into my car I felt irritated and defensive. It took me the whole trip to the hospital to settle down, rethink my priorities as a pastor, and regain a sense of confidence that I was keeping the biblical balance between caring for the flock and going out after the lost. In the eyes of that particular member, however, I was off-balance, and nothing on my part would convince him that he was not somehow being neglected.

Teaching, Modeling, and Organizing

The pastor fulfills his leadership role in evangelism in three ways: by *teaching and preaching* evangelism from the Scriptures, by *modeling* evangelism in his life and ministry, and by *organizing* the congregation for evangelistic thrusts into the community. It is like a three-legged stool, which will not stand unless all three legs are in place. All three carry their price, but not one can be neglected, or the ministry as a whole will suffer.

I have found repeated inspiration in an old book entitled *Pastor and Evangelist* by Charles L. Goodell. Writing about the pastor-evangelist's outlook, Goodell says the following:

> The lost man, like the lost sheep, does not come home of himself. He has to be sought. It is not enough to build your church and to stand in your pulpit and say "Come." You have to go out and seek, if you would save. When the passion for souls dies out, then all sense of the reality of religion perishes. It is when we see Him healing men that we have faith in the great physician; it is when we see the lost being saved that we believe in Christianity, and when the passion for the lost dies out in the pulpit, men will shiver around its cold ashes instead of warming their souls at the blaze of a light which was kindled in the heavens.
>
> Let us get then a clear conception of what the pastor is. The pastoral function is nothing more nor less than to watch over the sheep and to bring those who are straying back into the fold. Is it not time to go back to the one business for which the Church of God was organized and inspired?[1]

I can illustrate Goodell's argument in many ways. Early in the course of my pastorate in the United States, I encouraged a group of members to become involved in a coffee house ministry in the "skid row" area of the city. We soon had a convert, and he was as different from the ordinary church member as anyone could be. He had a long prison record and had once hijacked an airliner with 180 passengers on board to Havana, Cuba. He was tough as nails; but the

1. Charles L. Goodell, *Pastor and Evangelist* (New York: George H. Doran, 1922), p.110.

Lord melted his heart on the streets of the city, and one of our members, a seminarian, led him to repentance and faith in the gospel. I baptized him, and he became an active member of our church, and all the sermons I ever preached about missions and evangelism could not match the electrifying effect this man had on the congregation. Here was fresh and living evidence of God's mighty power to turn a sinner into a saint. From that point on I did not have to argue for the value of the coffee house ministry, because the proof sat in the audience every Sunday. And when I spoke of God's grace to "save a wretch like me," sinners up and down the scale of notoriety got the point that it was true.

Recently I visited a church I had pastored and with deep feeling watched a woman take holy communion. The first time I saw her I picked her up from the floor of a restaurant, where she had fallen from her chair. In her mid-fifties, dressed in furs, and obviously well-to-do, she was an alcoholic, widowed and lonely. The time was two days before Christmas, and she was having a hard time coping with her situation. Seated alone at a small table, she made the mistake of mixing too many drinks with the medication she was taking, and for a few moments she lost consciousness. But God had placed her table directly opposite ours. I picked her up and helped her out of the eating area. While a doorman brought her car to take her home, I talked with her and heard the outline of her story. She had been raised in a Christian home, married a non-Christian, and drifted from the church. Now widowed and without children, she was desperately lonely and hurting. Her heart yearned for the love of a caring community and the message of the good Shepherd who was still keeping a place in His sheep fold for her. She responded almost immediately to my words and started attending our church. Women of the congregation ministered to her, showing her love and support. A mid-week program for women seemed to fit her needs exactly. Now, several years later, she is a visibly changed person and is making steady progress in discipleship.

What does it take to be a pastor-evangelist? Not much, really, except a pastor's heart that loves sheep and seeks them redemptively wherever they are found. Even on a restaurant floor.

Other chapters in this book deal with conceptual issues relating to pastoral evangelism and present a series of practical applications for the pastor and congregation. In the final chapter I will return to my basic proposition that in order to fulfill the evangelistic duties inherent in the office, a pastor must teach and preach evangelism, model it in his own life, and organize the members to utilize their gifts for outreach. I am convinced that the evangelization of the world depends on the recapturing of this essential, biblical dimension.

I began this chapter with an illustration drawn from Sri Lanka, the scene of my first missionary pastorship; I conclude it in the same way with an example of bold witness by a pastor and some of his members. I was there when it happened, but I am indebted to my colleague, Clarence Van Ens, for some of the details of the story that he alone could supply.

In 1959, the prime minister of Sri Lanka, Solomon West Ridgeway Dias Bandaranaike, was shot dead by a Buddhist monk on the verandah of his home. The assassin's name was Talduwe Somarama, forty-five years of age, a man devoutly committed to his race, religion, and the Sinhala language. He and other monks had actively supported the prime minister's election campaign in exchange for political promises designed to further the cause of Buddhism. Once elected, the prime minister reneged on his promises, and Somarama was assigned to assassinate him. Clothed in his monk's robes, Somarama approached the unsuspecting official on the verandah of his home and shot him four times with a large caliber revolver. In his confession, Somarama declared, "I have done this thing to a man who did me no wrong for the sake of my religion, my language and my race." After trial, the judge sentenced him to die by hanging.

The assassin, however, was reached and saved by Christ before he was hanged. Naturally Somarama was the object of nationwide attention and was held in the country's tightest prison. But there were a pastor and a group of church members who felt burdened for his soul. They began praying for him. Conditions at the prison were such that Somarama was allowed to receive a Bible in the Sinhalese language, a continual flow of printed sermons and other Christian literature, and visits by a pastor. During the months before the execution, literature and conversations focused on the stark difference between Buddhism, which offers no forgiveness to anyone, and Christianity, which proclaims Christ the Savior and promises full remission of sins to all who repent and believe.

Twenty-four hours before he was hanged, Talduwe Somarama was baptized a Christian. Asked by news reporters why he, a former Buddhist monk, wanted to become a Christian, he replied, "I need forgiveness of my sins, and only Christ offers it." The next day he mounted the scaffold and was hanged. The press sensationalized the event, including his conversion. Many Buddhists rushed to obtain Christian literature, while others pressed for a stop to prison evangelism.

Five other prisoners, some of them notorious criminals, followed Somarama's example and asked for baptism. What led to this remarkable series of conversions? God's grace, of course, and the saving power of His Word; active lay people, members of a church beginning to experience renewal through evangelism activity; and a pastor burdened for lost sinners, willing to take risks and do the unordinary—even sitting with open Bible with an assassin in a jail cell. Jesus uses people like that.

___ 2 ___

Kingdom Evangelism
Edmund P. Clowney

In his recent book, *Evangelism: Doing Justice and Preaching Grace,* Harvie Conn warns us of the peril of the assignment I now undertake. One of the more common ways of avoiding evangelism is to escape to the study and write about it. That default can be compounded by lecturing on the theory of evangelism. Books and lectures on the subject can equip another crop of students to debate the issues, write committee reports, advance ecumenical dialogue, and discover still other fascinating substitutes for doing the work of an evangelist.

Of course, Harvie Conn's charge to go to the streets, not to the study, is found in a book that he wrote in his study. His book, however, is written in a style engaging enough to be read in the street. His purpose, like mine, is to coach theologians in the *practice* of evangelism and to see them doing it. As we consider in this chapter a theology for evangelism, we are not substituting reflection for witness. Sound doctrine expresses, after all, our grasp of the gospel we proclaim! It prepares us to preach and moves us to pray that the Lord of the harvest will thrust forth His laborers.

To deepen our understanding of evangelism we must deepen our understanding of the evangel. It is the gospel of the kingdom that must be proclaimed in all the world. Dispensational theology removes the gospel of the kingdom from the present age. In theory, if not often in practice, the dispensationalist puts the content of the synoptic Gospels on the shelf until the church age is over. The outworking of this misconception has affected evangelism in the

United States and around the world. Yet the error has not been fatal for at least two reasons. First, even if dispensationalism limits the theology of the church to the prison epistles of Paul, it does not find there a different gospel. Paul's theology is shaped throughout by the perspective of the kingdom, even if he seldom uses the term. Second, all but the most extreme dispensationalists have shown a happy inconsistency. The Scofield Bible tells us not to use the Lord's Prayer, since it is not for this age. But in this, as in many things, American "Bible" churches are more fundamentalist than dispensationalist. Scofield notwithstanding, they pray, "Thy kingdom come. Thy will be done in earth, as it is in heaven."

Reformed theology, on the other hand, has recognized the importance of the kingdom message of the Gospels, though admittedly, the Reformation, too, focused on Pauline theology, and the distinctive emphasis of the synoptic Gospels was not always appreciated. Enriched in recent years by the writings of Geerhardus Vos and Herman Ridderbos, Reformed scholars have come to see afresh the importance of biblical theology and, therefore, of the kingdom perspective. Continuing in this direction, I want to discuss in this chapter the meaning of evangelism as the proclamation of the gospel of the kingdom.

Kingdom Evangelism—Proclaiming the Lord

The good news of the kingdom is the announcement that the time is at hand for the fulfillment of the promises of God. The kingdom theme of the Gospels is drawn especially from the prophecies of Isaiah, Daniel, and the Psalms. The force of *basileia*, as has often been pointed out, is blunted by our word, "kingdom." The term, as we use it, suggests a realm, but the term in the Gospels describes the power of the king rather than the territory over which that power is exercised. The kingdom of God expresses His dominion rather than His domain. As the Psalms often affirm, God is King over all (Ps. 10:16; 29:10; 95:3). He is sovereign in all His ways and works. But more specifically, He is King in the midst of His people. He rules in Mount Zion (Ps. 9:11; 48:1-14; 50:2). God's kingdom in the special sense is His saving rule over His people. When God in His holiness judges His people for their sin, His kingdom promises are not forgotten. God will come again to deliver His people. All the prophets describe the saving rule of God in that great day. God will come to destroy not only the enemies of His people, but their sins (Mic. 7:18-20). Daniel describes the coming of the kingdom of God, a kingdom that will displace all other rule and stand forever (Dan. 2:44-45). God's kingdom will come with the coming of the Son of Man on the clouds of heaven (Dan. 7:13-14). To Him the eternal kingdom will be given. In the glory of His coming and by His power God will accomplish all that He has planned. The coming of the kingdom is the self-assertion of God in all His works.

The total sovereignty of God's action in bringing in His kingdom means that the kingdom is not something we prepare for God. The only sense in which we can "prepare the way of the Lord" is to cry out in repentance and faith. The "rending of the heavens" (Isa. 64:1) by which God will come to establish His kingdom, the fire of judgment, and the framing of the new creation are not man's work to perform. And yet the coming of the kingdom is not dreadful news, but good news; good news because God purposes salvation for His people. The promises of the Old Testament are so great that only the Lord Himself can fulfill them. If the kingdom of God is to come, the King must come. The angels announce to the shepherds that the baby in the manger is Christ, the Lord. He has come to save His people from their sins.

The Gospels all center on Jesus Christ. He is the Lord, the King; God's salvation is found in Him. He speaks as no man has spoken, not just because of the wisdom of His words, nor even just because He reveals His Father, but because of the way His words witness to Himself. He calls men to leave all and to follow Him; He reveals His power by mighty works, the very works of the Lord, whose path is in the sea, and who gives bread in the wilderness, sight to the blind, life to the dead (Isa. 35:3-5). When He calls His disciples to evangelism, He gives them a sign of His royal power. Before He promises to make them fishers of men, He fills their boats to the sinking point with fish (Luke 5:1-11).

Jesus is the Son of Man promised in Daniel. He speaks of the day when He will come on the clouds of heaven in the glory of His

Father, and with the holy angels. Yet in the garden of Gethsemane, when soldiers come to arrest Him, He does not summon legions of angels. The kingdom is present, because the King is present, yet the kingdom is to come because His *parousia* is to come. By His miracles, by His words, Jesus shows Himself to be the King. But by the restraint of His ministry He reveals the program of His kingdom. He did not come to bring the judgment but to bear it. The fire with which He baptized was not the fire of eternal destruction, but the fire of the Spirit. He called His disciples to take up their cross and follow Him. He promised them tribulation in the world, yet told them that He had overcome the world. In the life, death, and resurrection of Jesus the power of the kingdom is seen to be the power not of men, but of God.

Christ is Lord, not in spite of His sufferings and death, but in the triumph of His passion. His cross bore His royal title, and Jesus died as King. In Him God triumphed over the principalities and powers. Jesus cried, "It is finished!" and in that shout He accomplished the redemption of all those that were given Him of the Father. The authority at the right hand of God that Jesus exercises as the God-man is authority grounded in His victory on Calvary. His power as the King and Priest of glory guarantees the fulfillment of the purpose of His saving death, and of the restoration of all things.

Lordship Evangelism

Kingdom evangelism glorifies the Father in His Son, our Lord. It is lordship evangelism. Jesus Christ is held forth as Lord: Lord on the cross and on the throne. Evangelism calls men and women to become disciples of the Jesus of the Gospels. We are given the testimony of the Spirit to Jesus in the New Testament so that we might know Him and trust Him. We dare not invent new Christs of the "Indian road," or reprogram Jesus for the computer age. Our hope lies in the real Jesus, the Jesus of history and of faith. It is impossible to abstract from Jesus His role as Savior, and to claim His work in that capacity while withholding the total commitment to His lordship that He requires of those who would follow Him. It is the *Lord* whom we meet in the Gospels, the very Lord of glory. We cannot negotiate with Him; we cannot admit Him to our lives on our own terms, or invite Him to round out the religious dimension of a full life. How fearful is the temptation to view the Gospels as offering us resources from which we may draw material to construct a figure of Jesus for our purposes—however devout or sophisticated. Evangelism worships the Lord and hears His Word. It dare not package Jesus.

Kingdom evangelism will shrink back from other techniques of accommodating Christ's lordship to our control. Strangely, this is sometimes done in the name of that very lordship. Jacques Ellul has pointed out that the affirmation of Christ's lordship over history is sometimes used to sacralize history. The older liberalism worshiped at the shrine of "progress" and identified social progress with the rule of Christ. In another way, liberation theology repeats this mistake with a different ideal. It again claims to read off God's purposes from history and asks, What is the Lord doing in the world today? Liberation theologians may acknowledge that Jesus, during His earthly ministry, refused to allow His disciples to use the sword to establish His rule. Yes, He did refuse to lead them in revolt against Rome. But now, they maintain, the Lord's agenda can be seen to have changed; His purpose has moved with the progress of history. Revolution is now His work of salvation, the way He delivers the poor from their oppressors.

It is true that Christ as the Lord of history governs all things to the accomplishment of His plan. His present judgments do anticipate the final judgment of His power. From the throne of glory He executes His sentence upon the blasphemy of a boastful Herod (Acts 12:23), or of a lying Ananias (Acts 5:5). But Christ does not call upon His people to become His avenging angels. Peter may not draw the sword against Herod or Ananias. It is one thing to recognize the Lord's judgments in history; it is another to conclude that we are now called to implement them. Indeed, because the Lord withholds His full judgment till He comes, His providential rule of all things is still mysterious to us. As it is Christ who opens the seven seals of the book of God's decrees, we cannot claim to understand the total pattern of His judgments.

In ecumenical theology the lordship of Christ has been used to create a "worldly" doctrine in yet another way. The universalism of the atonement has long been assumed in reports prepared for the ecumenical movement. Since Christ died for every individual, and since His death was savingly effective, all men are saved. It is the world, therefore, that is in Christ. The church differs from the world only in possessing the knowledge of the world's salvation. Based on this reasoning, "openness to the world" has been advocated, a worldly theology that calls the church to identify with the world and to deal with the world's agenda. Joseph Sittler, of the University of Chicago Divinity School, gave an address to the Assembly of the World Council of Churches meeting in New Delhi in 1961 in which he called for a "cosmic Christology." The address has been seen as marking a turning point in World Council theology as it moved to deal with "worldly" concerns.

All such theories have the effect of making the kingdom of Christ a kingdom of this world. The separation wrought by the gospel of the kingdom is denied. Jesus said, not to the world, but to His disciples, "Fear not, little flock; for it is your Father's good pleasure to give you the kingdom" (Luke 12:32, KJV).

Jesus Christ is indeed Lord of the world. In His present glory He is in control not only of the cosmic galaxies, but also of the principalities and powers, the hosts of darkness that have been defeated at Calvary. In His future *parousia,* Jesus will be revealed as the Lord of judgment. Michelangelo's vast painting at the front of the Sistine Chapel celebrates Renaissance humanism and the painter's virtuosity, but biblical teaching underlies the scene. Christ is the mighty Judge who will declare at last the destiny of every created being. That is not only true—it is essential to the gospel. Hear the apostle Paul addressing the sophisticated Athenians on Mar's Hill. He preaches a kingdom evangel: the true and living God is sovereign, and God has intervened in history, calling upon all men everywhere to repent. What is the sign of God's calling men to account? "For [God] has set a day when he will judge the world with justice by the man he has appointed. He has given proof of this to all men by raising him from the dead" (Acts 17:31).

According to the gospel, Christ the cosmic Lord is the Judge. His judgment will bring division, and that division has already begun.

Jesus said that He came not to bring peace, but a sword (Matt. 10:34). Christ rules over all things; there are no boundaries or limits to His power. But He rules over all to redeem those who have been given Him of the Father: the little flock to whom the Father will give the kingdom. We must not fail to distinguish between the providential rule of Jesus Christ and His saving rule. Jesus is Lord of the church as well as Lord of the world, but the two senses of His lordship are not interchangeable. He controls the world now and will subdue every enemy in His final judgment. But Jesus already subdues us to Himself in another way; He triumphs over us by His rule of grace.

To speak of Christ's rule over the church as a saving rule does not, however, mean that it has no other purpose or meaning but to deliver us from judgment in the last day. Christ's saving purpose is total. He exercises total lordship to accomplish His purpose. His saving power is, of course, no less than His providential control of all things. It includes all that Christ does by His Word and Spirit to nurture and discipline us, to guard and keep us, to use us in His service, to conform us to His image. On the other side, our acknowledgment of His lordship must be total. We cannot dedicate a segment of our life to the Lord—the religious portion, for example. The basic requirement of the kingdom is that Christ shall be King of our lives, without qualification or exception. The Reformed faith has constantly emphasized the "world-and-life" view that Christ's lordship demands. Our service of Christ must be as inclusive as life itself. That service not only will determine the inclusion or exclusion of activities, it will also lead us to examine how we live and serve as lawyers, laborers, farmers, business people, or homemakers. The pattern of our obedience to Christ in the many spheres of life will form our own interpretation of the gospel. We are called to put the Word of Christ into the context of our living, individually, and as a community.

The "Holistic" Focus of Kingdom Evangelism

It is in this sense of Christ's rule that evangelism must be "holistic." We are redeemed by Christ, body and soul, and we are to serve

Him, body and soul. No activity of life, no decision, can remain out of His control. The gospel message, therefore, must demand total surrender to Christ. And yet, the gospel *promise* is no less inclusive. The renewal of Christ's salvation ultimately includes a renewed universe. In the meantime, there is no part of our existence that is untouched by His blessing. Christ's miracles were miracles of the kingdom, performed as signs of what the kingdom means. Jesus cared about the hunger of the crowds who heard His teaching. He commanded His disciples to give them food, and then miraculously furnished them with the resources to do so from the minuscule provision they could produce. Most of the miracles of Christ were miracles of healing. As signs they pointed to the divine power of Christ. But as signs they also pointed to His compassion, and the scope of His saving purpose.

The imagery of the miraculous signs was explained by the words of Christ. He came to call not the righteous, but sinners. His blessing was pronounced upon the poor, the afflicted, the burdened and heavy-laden who came to Him and believed in Him.

Kingdom evangelism must reflect the pattern of the kingdom as it is revealed in the words and deeds of Jesus. The miraculous signs that attested Jesus' deity and authenticated the witness of those who transmitted the gospel to the church are not continued, for their purpose is fulfilled. But the pattern of the kingdom that was revealed through those signs must continue in the church. We cannot be faithful to the words of Jesus if our deeds do not reflect the compassion of His ministry. Kingdom evangelism is therefore holistic as it transmits by word and deed the promise of Christ for body and soul as well as the demand of Christ for body and soul.

Kingdom evangelism must, of course, respect the program of the kingdom. Christ has promised us resurrection bodies at His coming. He has not promised us those bodies now. Rather, He has promised that through many afflictions we will enter the kingdom of God. But Jesus has shown His tender concern for our suffering bodies, and as the Lord of glory He still answers prayer.

Doxological Evangelism

We have seen that kingdom evangelism proclaims the Lord, God the Father and God the Son. For that reason it is triumphant and joyful. Because the kingdom has come and is coming, because God's will is being done, and Christ is Lord of Lords, our evangelism celebrates the kingdom of grace as it anticipates the kingdom of glory. Kingdom evangelism is doxological evangelism. If that note is not struck, no amount of evangelistic organization or technique will be adequate for the message.

Doxological evangelism cannot be catalogued with a host of worthy evangelistic methods: friendship evangelism, hospitality evangelism, evangelism in depth, personal evangelism, mass evangelism. It is not a technique. Humming a hymn may be a useful way to begin an evangelistic conversation, but doxological evangelism does not describe the importance of hymns in evangelistic campaigns, great as that may be. Rather, to speak of evangelism as doxological expresses the goal of evangelism, which must affect its very nature. Peter writes to the gentile church, "But you are a chosen people, a royal priesthood, a holy nation, a people belonging to God, that you may declare the praises of him who called you out of darkness into his wonderful light" (I Pet. 2:9).

In declaring that we are chosen as God's people to set forth His praise, Peter is citing a passage from Isaiah (43:21). There the Lord describes the blessings He gives to "my chosen, the people I formed for myself that they may proclaim my praise." The gospel message is celebration before it is communication. To proclaim God's praise is to enumerate His blessings, to describe the wonder of what God has done for us. The whole panorama of God's salvation of His people in the Old Testament provides a picture of our gospel witness. We are the redeemed of the Lord, delivered from bondage to the powers of darkness, brought to the city of God, where God Himself is with us. Now we sing to His praise and call the nations to join us in glorifying the only Savior in all the earth. The language of the psalms is evangelistic in this way. God is praised before the peoples, and all are called to come to join in singing His praise (Ps. 117:1; 47:1; 100:1; 105:1-3).

In the Old Testament the center for God's praise was Mount Zion; the prophets picture the nations streaming into Zion to glorify God the Savior-King (Isa. 2:2-4; 56:6-8). In the New Testament Jesus brings the fulfillment of that picture. No longer is Jerusalem the center for worship, for Christ is the true temple, and worship in spirit and in truth is worship in the Spirit that He gives, worship in Him who is the Way, the Truth, and the Life (John 4:21-26). We now come in worship to the heavenly Zion where Jesus is (Heb. 12:18-24). Because heaven is now the center for our worship, there can be no earthly sanctuary. The ascending Lord sends His disciples to the ends of the earth with the mission of calling the nations to join the saints and angels in heaven's praise. Surely it is not accidental that praising churches are so often growing churches. Evangelism is well practiced as God's people sing "How Great Thou Art!"

An Evangelism of Power

Kingdom evangelism rejoices in the saving work of God. It is conducted in power, in the full assurance of the work of the Holy Spirit (I Thess.1:5). Because it is doxological, it is far removed from the half-ashamed timidity that so often cripples our witness to the Lord.

As we have seen, kingdom evangelism is God-centered. The kingdom is the rule of the Father and of the Son, specifically the saving rule of divine grace. In the kingdom focus on God we are also directed to God the Holy Spirit. Jesus proclaims the kingdom in the power of the Spirit. He is anointed with the Spirit, is filled with the Spirit, and will baptize with the Spirit. In one sense, the work of Jesus prepares for the coming of the Spirit. The disciples are to wait in Jerusalem for the promise of the Father. Kingdom evangelism awaits the fulfillment of Pentecost. Of course, the coming of the Spirit does not mean that Jesus is superseded. Jesus is filled with the Spirit, and the Spirit fills with Jesus. The Spirit is sent at Pentecost from the throne of the glorified Christ; in the Spirit, Christ Himself is present.

Kingdom evangelism is not only for God's glory, it is by His power. The Book of Acts describes the work of the Spirit in bearing witness to Jesus Christ. The mission of the church is guided and empowered by the Spirit. Until the Spirit comes, the mission cannot begin. When the Spirit comes, the mission cannot stop. Even when the disciples do not go out from Jerusalem, they are driven out by persecution. The command of the Spirit commissions the first missionary team (Acts 13:1-4). Guided by the Spirit, the message of the gospel is carried to the Gentiles, to Asia Minor, Greece, and Rome. The growth of the church can be described as the growth and victory of the Word. The Spirit uses the proclamation of the gospel to reach God's elect in every tribe and nation. Note how Paul describes the evangelization of Thessalonica in the first chapter of his first epistle.

Obviously the leading and power of the Spirit do not come as a substitute for growth in wisdom. The Spirit does not suppress prayerful reflection. Rather, the Spirit works in us growth in wisdom as we prove out in obedience what is pleasing to God. But just as obviously, there is no greater threat to kingdom evangelism than trust in our own resources rather than in the provision and blessing of the Spirit.

End-Time Evangelism

Kingdom evangelism focuses on the plan of God just as it does on the person and power of God. The proclamation of the kingdom in the Gospels announces the coming of a God-appointed time. As we have already seen, the kingdom is presented as both future and present. Evangelism that proclaims God's kingdom must always take account of the *time* of the kingdom. The coming kingdom is the kingdom of glory. Its sure approach must be proclaimed as an essential part of the gospel message. Both the warning and the hope of the gospel flow from the certainty of the kingdom to come. When Christ comes again, the perfect justice of His kingdom will be revealed and enforced. The gospel of the kingdom does not ignore or take lightly the oppression and exploitation by which men grind down the poor and the powerless. Yet the gospel does not summon us to bring in God's judgment. God will do that. No sin will escape the just judgment of the Lord. *Justice delayed is not justice denied when it is God who is the Judge.*

Apart from God's judgment, human rage against injustice can never be satisfied. If, after forty years, a Nazi war criminal is caught and executed, a measure of justice has at last been done. But does this represent adequate retribution for the agonies of thousands whom he tortured to death? Rage against injustice often fuels a revolutionary violence that creates new injustice. We may feel that the freed inmates of Dachau who killed some of their former guards were amply justified: they summarily executed murderers. But when we see the blood shed in the world's revolutions, we begin to hesitate. Only God knows the heart, and before His goodness all the world stands guilty and condemned. We must tell men that they are right in supposing that wickedness should be punished. At last it will be. But what of their own guilty rebellion against God in that day?

The warning of the gospel is severe and profound. Apart from the judgment due to us for our sin there would be little reason for the good news of salvation. But the gospel of the kingdom is good news. The message of the coming kingdom of glory assures us of a future that surpasses all our dreams. Jesus has returned to heaven, Peter declares, until "the times of restoration of all things" (Acts 3:21, ASV). When that time comes everything will be made new: we will have resurrection bodies in a restored universe.

It may be easy to let that hope grow dim, to ask with the scoffer, "Where is this 'coming' he promised?" (II Pet. 3:4). Indeed, there are those who are made uneasy by a vivid expectation of the kingdom to come. Is that not to look for pie-in-the-sky by and by? Does that not cut the nerve of endeavor for a better world here and now? If we look for God's justice and His new order, will we not be complacent with injustice in the status quo? But social and political activism that gains by dimming the hope of the kingdom to come betrays the gospel. To precisely the extent that we seek "final solutions" to the injustices we perceive, we invest our panaceas with a religious sanction that makes them idolatrous. Social situations can be improved; political pressures may be resisted; if a government fails to fulfill its function of protecting and preserving life, it may even be overthrown. But none of these efforts can be identified with the coming of the kingdom of God. The Bible uses the term "regeneration" for the new order that comes with Christ (Matt. 19:28). Until then, men and women are regenerated by God's power, and brought into the new community of the church. But it is misleading to speak of regenerated or redeemed social structures.

The reality of the coming kingdom helps us to understand the form of the presence of the kingdom. Daniel's visions see the kingdoms of this world emerging as beasts from the sea. In the Book of Revelation the city of this world is represented by Babylon. The author of Hebrews warns us that we have not here an abiding city but seek after that which is to come. We are pilgrims, journeying toward the city of God. That city has foundations, and it will endure. But until that city comes to us, we can never give religious devotion to any city. *We are registered aliens in Babylon, but Babylon is not holy, nor is it our true home.* We may never identify the gospel of the kingdom with party politics. In our highly politicized age it is easy to conclude that the only valid "incarnation" of our faith is political. But that is to forget that the Christian faith is theopolitical, and that the politics of the kingdom seeks the city to come.

Kingdom Guidelines for Determining Priorities

Jacques Ellul, in his book *The False Presence of the Kingdom,* refers to the scorn with which historians have described the "hair-splitting" debates of the Byzantine theologians while the Turks were surrounding their city of Constantinople. Ellul asks, "What, in the final analysis, is the really important thing for the whole of mankind—that Jesus is indeed the Christ?—or that the Turks defeated the Byzantines in the early fifteenth century?"[1] Ellul was responding to the criticism that Christians spend their time on things like liturgy and ministry when there are urgent questions: the situation in Algeria, for example, and accounts of torture there. Since Ellul wrote, the French have long since left Algeria. Perhaps that bit of perspective will help us to understand his further statement about the Byzantine theologians: "It was far more *urgent* to know who was the Christ than it was to protect a temporal city against an ephemeral invader."

1. Jacques Ellul, *The False Presence of the Kingdom* (1972), pp. 92f.

To recognize the supreme urgency of the kingdom of God is not to be indifferent to human need and suffering. To the contrary, the gospel of the kingdom, as we have seen, is a message of comfort for the poor and oppressed. The gospel truly promises the triumph of love, justice, and liberty. But the weapons by which we advance the cause of the gospel are spiritual weapons. As Paul reminds us, we do not fight as the world does, nor do we use worldly weapons (II Cor. 10:3-6). Our spiritual weapons are not therefore ineffective. To the contrary, they are mighty before God to the casting down of ideological strongholds. Military power is not the greatest force in the world. The power of God's truth is greater. The gospel and only the gospel can liberate men's hearts and minds. The gospel changes the very thoughts of the heart, bringing all thoughts into captivity to Christ.

Kingdom evangelism has its own urgency. Because we know the time is short, we strive to buy up every opportunity for service and witness. Jesus' command to His disciples in Gethsemane to watch is a command repeated in the New Testament (Matt. 24:42; I Thess. 5:6; II Pet. 3:4). Watchfulness and soberness go together. Spiritual sobriety means alertness and realism, in contrast to the befuddled and hallucinatory experience of drunkenness. To watch means to look for the coming of the Lord, but this implies the opposite of dropping everything to wait for Him. Instead, watchfulness means being "girded" for service—as Jesus says about the faithful servants who are watching for their Lord. We are to be fully occupied in the service of Christ as we wait for Him. Indeed, we are to prize the moments given to us to do His work until He comes. Far from encouraging indolence or indifference, watching heightens stewardship. The Lord is coming; He will ask if we have visited Him in prison, fed Him when He was hungry, ministered to Him when He was sick—all as we have served His brethren in the world (Matt. 25:31-46). Since our Lord delays His coming until the gospel has been preached to all the world and all His people have been gathered in, kingdom evangelism has a special orientation toward the future (Matt. 24:14).

Kingdom Evangelism as Church Evangelism

Evangelism is the great kingdom mission of the church of Jesus Christ. When Peter confessed that Jesus was the Christ, the Son of the living God, Jesus said that Peter's confession was God-given, and that upon the confessing Peter as an apostolic rock, He would build His church (Matt. 16:18-19). Jesus then gave authority to Peter (and in Matt. 18:18 to all the disciples), the authority of the keys of the kingdom. There is therefore a close connection between the church and the kingdom. The authority of the church of Christ is authority with respect to the kingdom of God. The church cannot be identified with the kingdom for the very reason that the kingdom is so centered on God. It is the sphere of God's saving power, not a community of men and women. To confuse the church with the kingdom would be like confusing the saved with the Savior. But the church is the community of the kingdom. It is the company of those who by grace are made heirs of the kingdom of glory and who have been delivered from the power of darkness and transferred into the kingdom of the Son of God's love (Col. 1:13). As those who have been brought under Christ's lordship, the members of His church have a kingdom witness in two perspectives.

First, the church is the *diaspora* of the kingdom: the people of God scattered in the world. They are, as we have seen, pilgrims and aliens, having no abiding city here. But they are also ambassadors. They are seen as lights in the world, and they are scattered in order that their witness might be effective. They will meet with opposition and persecution. In the world they will be called upon to suffer for Christ's sake. But such opposition will only offer further occasion for their witness. They must be prepared, when they are questioned or accused, to give a reason for the hope that is in them (I Pet. 3:15). Their scattering will come partly through persecution, partly through the circumstances of their lives; but there is a more compelling reason: the church is sent forth by Jesus to carry His name to the ends of the earth. To be sure, not all Christians are apostles, and not all Christians are evangelists; there is a marked difference in gifts recognized in the New Testament. The preaching of the Word by those called to evangelistic ministry remains a primary means by which the gospel spreads. Yet every Christian must confess the name of Christ, and the whole church has fellowship in witness to Christ before the world. Certainly the lifestyle of the Christian community manifests to the world the meaning and reality of Christ's lordship. Christians become salt in the cultures of this world because their uprightness of life restrains the corruption of the world. But Christians are also lights. As men see their good works, they are summoned to glorify God, and to seek His grace for themselves.

The church is not only *scattered* in the world; it is also *gathered* in the world as the visible community of the people of God. Their gathering is not geographical like that of Israel. There is no holy land for God's people, nor a holy city in which they are called to live: not Jerusalem, or Rome, or Geneva—nor even Wheaton, Illinois! Yet the good news of the kingdom requires that the community of the kingdom should be manifest. As Jerusalem was a city set on a hill in the Old Testament, a city where God's glory was seen, and to which the nations were called, so now the church of Christ is a city set on a hill.

The Witness of Holiness, Compassion, and Proclamation

The church is called to be a holy community. If the church tolerates within itself the ethical abominations of the heathen world around, it loses its witness. Without careful shepherding and discipline the real nature of the church will not be made evident. The epistles of the New Testament make it clear that the apostles took most seriously the holiness of the life of the church. Paul's great burden was that he might present the church as a pure virgin to Christ (II Cor. 11:2). If the Galatians turned aside from the purity of the gospel, the apostle wrote to them in anguish of heart. If at Corinth the church tolerated a form of incest, the apostle warned in stern words and threatened yet sterner action. The very love of Christ that binds the church together will demand loyalty to the Word of Christ and to His commandments. No doubt the greatest obstacle to Christian witness in most communities where the church is established is the unrebuked sin of so many of its members. To those outside it may seem that the church is no different from the world.

As a city on a hill the church has open gates, not only to welcome in those who are drawn to worship, but also to go out in ministering service. The church is a diaconal community. Christians are charged to do good to all men, and especially to those who are of the household of faith. Christians are driven to serve others by the very nature of the gospel of the kingdom. The gospel is the story of God's free and gracious love. When God owed us nothing but the wrath of His just judgment, He gave His only begotten Son for us. In the parable of the Good Samaritan, Jesus pictures the love that fulfills the law of a gracious God. It is not a love that calculates, or that passes by on the other side, persuading itself that no obligation is present. On the contrary, the love that fulfills the law is love modeled on God's love: the love of compassion that sent Jesus into the world. We who have tasted God's free and undeserved love may never ask, "Who am I obliged to love? Who is my neighbor?" We know that we were loved by God when it would seem that He was, rather, obliged to hate us as His enemies. If He loved us when we were His enemies, we must love those who are now ours. If He forgave the vast debt of our sin, how readily should we forgive others! If He sought us when we were in the far country, how ready we should be to seek others and call them to come home! Mission is built into the very meaning of the gospel. If we fail to see it, we should ask if we understand the message of pure, sovereign grace.

God's compassionate love in Christ constrains us. We must follow Him who came to seek and to save that which was lost. Our ministry of mercy shows the compassion of Christ: it cannot be limited to words when we meet the world's wounded on the Jericho road. Word and deed go together in kingdom evangelism, for the King is our Lord, and we go in His name.

In the perplexities that we face as His missionary church, His lordship is our hope. It is the key that opens our understanding: in no other way can we reconcile our modeling of His justice while acknowledging that the judgment is His at His return. Praise His name, Christ's lordship is more than the key to our understanding. It is that sovereignty of Him who is both the Lamb and the Lion. To many it seems absurd to suppose that Christ should establish a kingdom that is not of this world, and refuse to let His servants fight to bring it in. How else can evil be restrained, tyranny overthrown, and righteousness established? The answer, of course, is that Christ has all power, in heaven and earth. His judgments even now control the raging of the nations. He leads His pilgrim people by paths that they do not yet understand to the day when all the kingdoms of this world shall become His kingdom of glory.

_ 3 _

Prayer and Evangelism
C. John Miller

I come to this subject with joy and fear and trembling. Anyone who writes on the subject of evangelism ought to have fear and trembling, and anyone who writes on the subject of prayer ought to be scared to death. Just what happens when evangelism takes place is a bit of a mystery. And when prayer takes place, that's a greater mystery. I don't mean it is so foggy you can't define it, but these things are certainly done in the wisdom and power of God, and are not of men. Appropriately, then, we approach these subjects with prayer, asking God for His presence.

God, our Father, how we thank You that Jesus Christ is our fellowship with You. We thank You that, as our mediator, He knows all about You and He knows all about us. And when we pray, He's really the one bringing us together, and we discover that strange things do happen to us. Our minds are clarified. Our hearts are softened. Our sense of life and reality is renewed. Our openness to the Scriptures is increased. And we also see, Lord, that You are pleased to take our prayers, and that You are willing out of Your great kindness to use them as the vehicle for fulfilling Your will on the earth; that when we pray for the salvation of the lost, You hear our prayer, and men are convicted of sin, believe, and so confess with their lips and are saved. We marvel at this! We also marvel that in prayer we find ourselves in partnership with the living God; that You have ordained that we should be the instruments in prayer of the realizing and fulfilling of Your will on the earth; and that You have indeed called us as part of Your family so that when we pray we do not come as orphans, but we come to our own Father. We thank You that, though we are sinners by nature, are alienated from You in life and heart, and have minds darkened by evil, You were pleased by Your loving-kindness to bring us into Your household and give us Your Spirit, whereby we cry, "Abba, Father." And so we thank You for Him, and we pray that, even as we approach this subject, as we lay our minds open to Scripture, as we review things that are crucial principles, You would guide us. May this study turn into a new closeness to our God, a new assurance of His love, a new power for our personal witness, a new freedom in all our relationships, a new tenderness, a new compassion, a new perceptiveness. May it give us increased freedom in the Spirit and bring much glory to Your name. We ask it in the authority of Jesus' name. Amen.

Books on Prayer

I'd like first to mention a few books to advance your knowledge of prayer. As I stated earlier, prayer is a kind of mystery. Oftentimes and in many ways we have vague notions about prayer, and we don't quite know how to pray; we can listen to lectures or we can try to pray, and yet we feel very ineffective. Sometimes it's difficult even to evaluate, Did I pray or didn't I pray? In my *Evangelism and Your Church* is a bibliography with a section on prayer. I list there a book called *Prayer* by O. A. Hallesby. In this book he talks about just this kind of mystery; he goes so far as to say that even a groan from a Christian heart may prove to be a significant prayer before God. I happen to know that Hallesby's book has widely influenced Christians, giving them more confidence that even their feeblest efforts can have a place in the presence of God.

I'd also commend to you, on the personal side of prayer, a book by Mrs. Howard Taylor, *Behind the Ranges*. I would especially call your attention to chapter 11. If you are planning to be a pastor or a missionary you ought to know chapter 11 well. It's a missionary-pastoral classic, especially for those who are engaged in pioneer work.

If you want something else on that personal side of prayer, read

Calvin's *Institutes,* Book 3. I think it contains the best material ever written on prayer. Other books are perhaps very familiar to you, for example, E. M. Bounds's *Power Through Prayer.* Perhaps a less well-known book, valuable to generations of Christians for its humbling effect, is one by Austin Phelps. If you ever think you know how to pray and are lifted up in pride, I would suggest you get a copy of Austin Phelps's *The Still Hour* or *Communion With God.* Every time I feel I am getting arrogant, I go back and look at that book, and Phelps tells me about all the idols I carry to prayer. This book has depressed generations of Christians, yet it is a very valuable book because it humbles us and teaches us important things about prayer.

And there is, of course, Andrew Murray's *With Christ in the School of Prayer,* for my money, one of the best things Andrew Murray has written. It's especially strong on what it means to pray in the name of Christ, to God as Father. Also I commend to you Eremeus's *Jesus' Promise to the Nations,* also listed in the bibliography of *Evangelism and Your Church.* I have found this book most influential. Not that I agree with his neoorthodox eschatology, but it has some needed material.

In the area of corporate prayer, a great classic you should rush to the library and get is Jonathan Edwards's *An Humble Attempt to Promote Explicit Agreement and Visible Union of God's People in Extraordinary Prayer for the Revival of Religion and the Advancement of Christ's Kingdom.* That isn't the book, that's just the title. This particular book is probably the single most important book on prayer in America because of its great influence historically in the revivals of the eighteenth, nineteenth, and early twentieth centuries. Much of the massive religious shift that came to the United States in 1858 and 1859 came because people had read this, or had at least heard ideas from it, and had engaged in concerts of prayer. Basically it contains an exegesis of the last two or three verses in Zechariah 8.

On corporate prayer, I commend Harvie Conn's "Luke's Theology of Prayer," in *Christianity Today* (December 22, 1972). If you want to read about the history of corporate prayer during the Great Awakening, read *The Fervent Prayer* by J. Edwin Orr. It is a very significant piece of work.

Why Pray?

As we think now about prayer, I'd like to begin with our need, or our perceived sense of need, or the opening of the mind to learn new things. When Harvie Conn, Jay Adams, Ed Clowney, and I were in the practical theology department at Westminster Theological Seminary (it's difficult to imagine all those people in one department, but there we were, and rarely did we ever agree on anything), somebody one day said, "If there were one thing we could give our students at Westminster, what would that be?" Amazingly, without much discussion, we reached complete agreement: "If we could give each student the power to engage in constructive self-criticism . . ." And that's really what we are concerned about here, a constructive looking at yourself. Just pray where you really are, not where you think you are; often there can be a wide gap between those two.

I remember in 1967, when I first began seriously to question my own ability to pray. I tried to engage in constructive self-criticism. I was preaching during that summer in a small church in eastern Pennsylvania, and I felt some deep inadequacies in my preaching that needed changing. And you'll come to that, if you become a pastor, sooner or later. If you can come to it sooner rather than later, it will be a great blessing to you and the church. I came to mine rather late; I had been in the ministry about seven years when I decided I had a problem in stating the gospel clearly and succinctly. I had led people to Christ in living rooms and various other places, but I was not sure that anyone had ever become a Christian through my preaching. I decided that was a weakness, and I worked on it. I also had trouble getting people to see their need. My preaching might have been relevant in another century, something like the seventeenth. It didn't seem to do what I thought it should, and so I decided when all else had failed—pray.

I didn't know much about prayer. By this time I had my Ph.D. and all those years at Westminster and other training, but the more I learned, the less able I seemed to be to pray. I couldn't figure it out, but I decided that every Saturday afternoon I was going to take my sermon and go somewhere by myself and pray and see what would happen. And the truth of the matter was that I had a little bit of the spirit of Zechariah the priest who prayed for a son and was silent when he got the answer.

Well, I prayed fervently. The next morning was Mother's Day, and I let go. My preaching didn't really seem much different, except that when I got to the door of the church, there were two women there. They were strangers—they tend to show up on Mother's Day. I had the right day for my particular text. My wife came up to me afterwards and said, "Did you notice the two women? They had tears in their eyes." I said, "What do you make of it?" and she said she didn't know. Sunday evening came around, and they came back to church with Bibles—big Bibles! It was obvious they were not accustomed to being in church. They didn't have Bibles in the morning, but they had dug out the family Bibles, which told us all of this was not familiar to them. And there they were.

Later, I called on them and found out what happened. One of them said, "We both were converted in that service. We came in with one theology, and one concept of what salvation is all about, and everything you said applied to us, and we suddenly realized that we had it all backwards. We thought salvation came as a result of what you did, not as a result of Christ's blood." God had converted them both. It startled me that two people were saved! Though I had prayed fervently on Saturday, "God, save some people on Sunday," I preached with little faith, but the result was that two people were converted. Obviously God had prepared them. He had heard the prayer; He brought them there, and they were convicted of sin, came into the kingdom, and became members of the church. That was enough to alarm me. Maybe there was more to this praying than I thought I knew.

My basic philosophy had been, why pray when you can worry? Many seminary graduates develop that kind of ministerial philosophy very quickly. But the suspicion that came to me was, "Maybe other Christians know something I don't know." Now that's hard for a Westminster man to admit. In fact, in that particular church was a lady who sat in the front row and prayed very fervently for me every Wednesday night. I can remember being baffled by that. I said to myself, "Doesn't she know that I have gone to Westminster

Seminary?" And then the thought occurred to me, "Maybe this is what she does know." So much for the onset of creeping humility.

I decided at that point that in this whole matter of need, or just discerning where things were, of getting aboard, to visit some other Christians God was using, to see how His kingdom power moved among them. I visited an inner-city pastor in Newark, New Jersey—Grover Wilcox. I also spent some time with the Schaeffers at L'Abri. I visited a person led to the Lord and commended to me by Martyn Lloyd-Jones—a Miss Elizabeth Brond in a slum area of London.

As I visited these people, I found some common features in all their work. One, they labored to make the gospel clear and relevant. They really did labor, all four of them. Two, I discovered that these people who were having many conversions and seeing lives transformed were also available people. They were on the spot. They were out there where people were; they were sitting right in the middle of them. Three, they all put themselves in positions of vulnerability. A willingness to suffer was manifested in each of them. Four, they were all unusually effective in prayer. If you asked them if they were effective in prayer, they would no doubt have denied any special diligence. When I asked this of Grover Wilcox, he spent about ten minutes deploring his prayer life. Don't interpret that as meaning this man does not pray; I know he spent every Monday morning—the whole morning—in prayer.

I also had trouble getting a favorable response out of Miss Elizabeth Brond. So many young people were being converted in her part of London that the gangs had disappeared and the police came down to investigate, to find out what in the world that lady was doing. Not only did Martyn Lloyd-Jones tell me about her, but also Ken Campbell, a Westminster student from Scotland, told me about her. I said, "All right, what is it that's moving here in the kingdom? There is a power of God here. She doesn't look like my idea of an evangelist." Ken said, "You ought to sit and listen to her pray. If you did, you'd have no doubt why people are turning to Christ." That was very convicting . . . very convicting.

When my wife and I spent time with the Schaeffers at L'Abri, we saw a side of them that sometimes is missed. The Schaeffers prayed all the time and about everything. They had days of prayer for which people signed up and then prayed at different times throughout the day. Every time they moved they were praying. They prayed before things; they prayed after things. And at that time, many, many conversions took place at L'Abri. It led me to see that I don't know how to pray very well.

Until I learn to pray well, I'll not be very effective in evangelism and witness. And yet, I believe you really never get to the place where you can say, "I know how to pray." I would be afraid of you if you told me you knew how to pray. I mentioned coming to the subject of prayer with fear and trembling, because you must be taught and renewed in prayer constantly by the head of the church. When the disciples came to Jesus and said, "Lord, teach us to pray," they went to the only one who can do that work. We can help people learn to pray, but we certainly cannot teach them. As Calvin said, prayer is always getting its fervor out of its sense of inadequacy.

The very thing that is strong in our Presbyterian tradition is that we want to develop our skills, we want to learn the tools. Nothing is wrong with that. We labor to make the gospel clear, we labor over our sermons, and we take preaching seriously. But how often we begin to think of ourselves and our backgrounds, our training, our gifts, and all the rest as providing a human adequacy! We lean on that which is visible: what we are, what we have done, or what we expect other people to do. In that state, we cannot pray effectively. The whole idea of prayer is that we call on the name of the invisible God. To come in prayer is to abandon everything, to claim God's promises, and to know God, not to know what we have to bring. I don't mean that praying is like taking a pistol and blowing out your brains every time you pray. But when you pray you stand on holy ground, and God alone has a right to set the terms of that meeting.

Four Principles

I'd like to relate this, by some foundational principles, to biblical evangelism. I will mention four that have to do with both prayer and evangelism.

First, when we pray about evangelism, we need a place to begin.

We have rightly emphasized in our tradition, although not strongly enough, that *evangelism and prayer begin with divine sovereignty.* The first foundational principle for effective prayer and evangelism is that we start with the divine sovereignty, the almightiness of our God. Now, that can be an abstraction. It can be almost as depersonalized as Spinoza's vision, but we mean something very concrete. We mean not only that in all things God is in control, that God has planned all things in His sovereignty and good pleasure from the beginning to the end, but also that God has put into history a mighty salvation. That makes all the difference in the world, when you say with Jonah, "Salvation is of the Lord." He's praying there, you see. The great theme of the Bible is salvation is of the Lord, and because it is of Yahweh, it is a sovereign, irresistible, almighty salvation.

When I'm praying, then, I'm not praying to a God who is not in the business of doing very much; I'm talking to the God who has a kingdom, and that kingdom comes and moves with power. In other words, sovereignty has appeared in our redemption. God has given us the gospel within the framework of His salvation and has said that the gospel and nothing else is the power of God unto salvation, so that when I pray and do evangelism, I have laid hold of God's own approach, God's own method. This gospel alone can deliver modern man from the world Kafka has described. If you think the law can do it, if you think your preaching can do it, if you think anything you can do will suffice, you're sadly mistaken. Only the gospel will suffice, and for that reason we pray with the apostle Paul that it may be presented boldly (Eph. 6:19-20) and that it may be made very clear (Col. 4:4).

If we have a mighty salvation, and the gospel is the way people lay hold of that salvation through faith, the heart of this sovereignty needs to find practical expression in prayer and witness. It's right here in Scripture, but it's the most deemphasized doctrine in our tradition. This sovereignty has to do with the ascension of our Lord Jesus Christ. If you're going to witness effectively, pray effectively, you have to be persuaded of Jesus' ascension and His present rule over all things. As the one at the Father's right hand, Christ is ready to give you the Holy Spirit, to teach you to pray, and to teach you to witness.

Notice how John 7 relates to Jesus' glorification. In verses 37-39 we read:

> On the last and greatest day of the feast, Jesus stood and said in a loud voice, "If a man is thirsty, let him come to me and drink. Whoever believes in me, as the Scripture has said, streams of living water will flow from within him." By this he meant the Spirit, whom those who believed in him were later to receive. Up to that time the Spirit had not been given, since Jesus had not yet been glorified.

The whole emphasis on the giving of the Spirit to the thirsty is a picture of need, prayer, and the claiming of a promise; that promise is based upon Jesus in glory, Jesus ascended in power, the one who gives the Spirit. Or to use the language of Peter in Acts 2:33, Jesus has "received from the Father the promised Holy Spirit" and "has poured out" or shed abroad the Spirit. It makes all the difference in the world when you are praying whether your prayers are feathers in the wind, whether you're pursuing multiple requests, or whether you see the central truth that Jesus Christ is an ascended Lord—Lord over the church and Lord over the world. He has all authority, and when you pray, you are in partnership with Him. If you learn that even a little bit, it will build your faith, which is then the very heart of evangelism and prayer. "All things are possible to him who believes. Be it according to your faith." That's the great cry of Scripture. If you pray, you must pray in faith. If you witness, you must witness in faith on the basis of a knowledge of the living, risen, ascended Lord.

The first time that dawned on me, I was about to give some lectures in a restaurant. I went in to case the joint before I gave the lectures. This was back in the days when hippies were new to that area, rather recently issued. I met one. He sat down right next to me where I was having my piece of pie before I went in to give my lecture. And he said, "What's going on in there tonight?" And I said, "Well, man," (I beat him to the punch), "it's like this, I'm speaking." "What's it all about?" he still wanted to know. I said, "Well, it's about Jesus. He's Lord, and we are going to be talking about Him." He looked at me, put down his utensils, and walked out the door. It dawned on me what had happened. I had talked as though Jesus were present and alive, and he believed me. He expected Jesus to come in the door, and he wanted to get out first. You may say that was just superstitious; Jesus really wasn't going to be there. How do you Know? Maybe He wasn't going to be there in the physical sense that this guy expected. But when we are witnessing, how many of us witness as though Christ was crucified, died, was buried, was raised, and then evaporated? Many talk that way. They neither expect Him to return, nor do they expect Him to do anything now.

The foundational principle of divine sovereignty must mean you have faith that the Holy Spirit is in the possession of Christ—the glorified Christ. Because of His mediatorial work, He now sheds Him abroad. The whole power in witness is that the Lord is risen. The Lord is alive. Jesus is coming back. If you don't have those things, you're half a Christian—you don't know about the ascension, you don't know about Pentecost. Doctrine becomes a museum-piece. That's not the way Scripture intended it to be.

Second, corporate and private prayer are the primary ways Christ's Spirit is communicated to us. Herman Bavinck says, in essence, that the Holy Spirit is assimilated to Jesus, and then He sheds Him forth. The way Christ acts, the vehicle He uses, the means He uses—is prayer.

Notice the language of John 14:12-14: "I tell you the truth. Anyone who has faith in me will do what I have been doing. He will do even greater things than these, because I am going to the Father." Notice the ascension here. When Jesus speaks, He says you will do the things I have been doing, and you will do greater things, because of the ascension—because He will be in the place of authority. And then He tells His listeners, "And I will do whatever you ask in my name, so that the Son may bring glory to the Father. You may ask me for anything in my name and I will do it." Now the picture here, dear brothers and sisters, is simply that we have this great promise, a staggering promise. The greater works are possible for Christians because Jesus in His glory is so great. And how is this communicated? This power is the instrumentality of the Spirit, Jesus working through us, and it comes by prayer. Obviously it is by authoritative prayer because it is asked in the name of the Son. And so on that basis we engage in corporate and private prayer, in order to claim what God has for us. Look back to the previous verse, "If any man thirst, let him come and keep coming, and let him drink." He who believes (that's the whole process), according to Scripture, "from within him shall flow rivers of living water." Paul, using somewhat different language, says in Philippians 1:19, "I know I am going to be delivered through their prayer and the supply of the Spirit."

Third, the vehicle of the Spirit's working is bold faith. I've already stated this principle, but I want to express it more clearly. Boldness of faith is ardent, confident faith, working through love. We've seen that divine sovereignty and corporate and private prayer are primary means for Christ's communicating the Spirit. The manifestation of the Spirit's working is in boldness of faith—faith in prayer, but also faith in deeds, in love, and in witness. We need to unpack that idea of boldness because we can easily misunderstand it and think of bold faith as merely intense. That is not always the case. I'm not offering a model that is necessarily flamboyant, but rather I am saying faith is ardent. This faith is essentially sure that Jesus is alive and that Jesus is Lord of history. It is sure too, that every time you meet someone, that meeting was appointed by Him, that these are not chance meetings, and that you are part of a great harvesting plan. When you pray for people, you are confident that His Spirit will be working.

Fourth, we are seeking not decisions, but disciples, self-consciously soliciting a commitment to glorify Jesus Christ by a changed life. We want to convict consciences. We want people to perceive the love of God. We want them to know about the promises, in order that they may by a changed life, by the difference between what they once were and what they have become in Christ, bring glory to God. I believe that means, among other things, becoming an active church member.

I do have one further point, and it is most crucial. If you study the Scriptures about prayer, you see it described as toil. In one sense prayer is waiting, resting, but in another sense it is toil. Paul uses the word *agōnia* (striving, even agony) in relation to prayer, and he seems to tie this into evangelism. In Galatians 4, he reflects on travailing in birth again with the Galatians. "Again" points back to an earlier travailing; when he saw these people, he travailed in prayer for them. He strove in prayer for them. And the same kind of striving was in his preaching. It wasn't a cold preaching; rather, it came spontaneously, and he preached only the cross, in order to give them the fullness of the gospel in what Christ had done, letting nothing stand in the way—and that takes agony.

I once asked one of the graduates of Westminster Seminary, one of the best preachers, I think, to have come through its halls, how he put together his sermons. He said, "I do it this way. I agonize over the meaning of every word in the text. I really sweat blood over it. I labor to get a good outline. I write the whole sermon out. And then when I go to the pulpit, I never take it with me." He said, "In the agony, there's a resting. I want nothing there but God that I depend on." So in a sense the agony is a coming to rest in God, paradoxical as that might seem. It is coming to see the power of the gospel in your own life and experience. You pray that these things may become clear to you so that when you come to preach you hit the target. We have so much preaching today, and so much witnessing, that goes around and around; and the law and the gospel, and the difference between them, don't come through clearly. We're fuzzy in these things. So the striving in prayer is not, as I stated earlier, to blow out our brains, but to clear our heads and get to the point.

The Nature of Prayer and Evangelism

Having said that, I would like to give some sharpened definitions of biblical prayer and evangelism. J. I. Packer said in *Evangelism and the Sovereignty of God* that, according to the New Testament, evangelism is just preaching the gospel—the evangel. I like that. It gets us to the heart of the matter. I know of a Reformed theologian who defined prayer almost the same way, except talking in a different direction. "Prayer is just talking to God my Father." I don't have a quarrel with either of those definitions, as far as they go. But if we now speak of "effective" prayer, "effective" evangelism (or what we might call normative new covenant prayer, normative new covenant evangelism), then we have added a dimension. Edwards strove for that dimension when he called for extraordinary prayer, but by extraordinary prayer he meant people meeting for several hours to pray. That's not exactly what I mean.

The New Testament uses some very strong words to describe both evangelism and prayer. We find one such word in Hebrews 10:19: "Therefore brothers since we have boldness to enter the most holy place by the blood of Jesus, by a new and living way. . . ." The boldness, the *parrēsia*, is freedom. The blood of Christ has taken away guilt. I have nothing to hide. I'm open. God has nothing against me. There's no offense any longer. I go reverently and daringly when I pray, when I draw near to God.

Paul uses similar terminology when he describes prayer and worship that isn't just talking to God, but is a son talking to God, a son who knows he belongs to his Father and takes to Him the desires of his heart. Paul also describes evangelism that way. In Ephesians 6:19-20, Paul says, "Pray for me, that whenever I open my mouth, words may be given me, so that I will fearlessly make known the mystery of the gospel for which I am an ambassador in chains. Pray that I may declare it fearlessly, as I should." The word translated "fearlessly" is the same word translated "boldness" in Hebrews 10:19. That particular word has in it the sense of a confident faith, no reservations, no fears. You are going, as it were, without any hesitancy into the presence of God and into the presence of people. You are an ambassador. "I am an ambassador in chains, so you pray for me. I will have courage. I will have confidence. I will have ardent faith." Donald McGavran says there are two things that make churches grow. One is natural bridges, such as hospitality and friendship, and the other is ardent faith. And so Paul says, "Help me now to take the gospel and make it known with ardent faith."

This takes us back to our first fundamental principle: we proclaim a sovereign salvation. Men may harden their hearts, and it becomes a savor of death to death; but they may believe, and it becomes a sweet savor to life. Whichever way it goes, the gospel is victorious, as part of a mighty salvation. Isn't that enough to get you excited? You see, you are not a little orphan going out to witness. The ardent faith isn't something you generated. God does not send you out to a vast orphan asylum, where you don't know your own name or anyone else's, but rather He sends you out knowing the power of the gospel—the power to convict men of sin; the power to take a dead conscience, defiant of God, and make it alive and sensitive, through the Spirit.

In Acts 4:13 the same word describes the apostles. The rulers and elders saw Peter and John as ignorant and unlearned men, and they marveled. What did they marvel about? Not that they were ignorant and unlearned men. There were plenty of ignorant and unlearned men around. We still have plenty of them. But they marveled because they saw the apostles' courage, their boldness. In Acts 4:23, after the apostles had gone through that ordeal, they prayed again that God would give them great boldness, and then they spoke the Word with great boldness.

I'm suggesting, then, that we have in prayer something more filial, something more of sonship, something more daring.

Our household was often very busy in times past; it still is sometimes. I would have people backed up wanting to see me. My son, when he came to visit me, always walked by everybody. He was married and no longer at home, but he walked by everybody, sat down next to me, and told me what was on his mind. People were always shocked by that; they wanted to know how he got away with that. I said, "Well, he's my son, he has a right here." It is the same with God. We preach as sons, those who know the Father, who are in friendship with Him. Christ's propitiation has taken away His wrath and has made us friends. God smiles on us with permanent approval. He even loves you. How could He? You know all the guilt you have floating around. I have it too, but He loves me. Amazing Grace!

Another such word is *plērophoria*. It means conviction, assurance. Used of witness in I Thessalonians 1:5 and again of worship in Hebrews 10:22, it describes prayer in the one case, and witness and evangelistic preaching in the other case. The whole idea is that in ministry a power and a presence is brought to bear when the Spirit is there. That power and presence is so strong that men are convinced God brought the preacher. If you never convince anyone that God brought you, don't preach. If God didn't bring you, if you didn't get something on you knees, if you weren't broken before the Word, what are you preaching for? You're asking other people to do what you don't do. If you don't know God very well, if you can't even learn anything about prayer, and you don't pray, then you shouldn't preach. Prayer and preaching go together. When we see prayer more as a partnership, it becomes much more enjoyable. You define the striving in relationship to a God who wants to give you the Holy Spirit, and when you join in corporate prayer, you see that He has officially, covenantally, committed Himself to give you the Holy Spirit.

Now you say, isn't that Arminianism? God isn't an Arminian, and He says in Matthew 18:19-20 that where two or three of you are, and you agree on anything (He's talking about church discipline in this case), He'll be there in your midst. We could even say that where the claiming of these promises is concerned, the church prays with one accord; as in Acts 1:13-14, when the New Testament church prays and Pentecost follows, we are together with one mind. One mind is the literal idea, one accord devoted to prayer. It was together, and in that togetherness, that God brought about Pentecost—it was during corporate prayer.

Edwards saw this, and when he wrote that little book with the long title that I mentioned earlier, he said, "Is there a promise here that the church has not effectively claimed?" He moved the whole definition of prayer away from just a human striving to a striving-claiming, claiming God's work in our day! He suggested concerts of prayer, people praying on Monday or on Saturday evening or on Sunday morning for revival. I want to stress that prayer in this partnership sense claims the promises and constitutes part of the essence of the life of the church.

Witnessing also expresses that same kind of faith. It has daring in it, boldness in getting the gospel through to people. It doesn't always mean that you have to stand up on something and yell. There might be times for that. But it might come in a very still, small voice, as it were. When I had my heart attack in Uganda (I don't recommend heart attacks anywhere, and definitely not in Uganda), as I was lying there, I thought, "This is the end." I was ready to say goodbye to the world when it finally dawned on me that maybe God wanted me to pray. I had forgotten all about prayer, all about the promises, all about Scripture; I couldn't think of one. I hate to admit that. A real prayer warrior could have prayed. But I couldn't. I had to pray for prayer. I said, "God give me grace. I'm not handling this well at all." And God heard that prayer. As I surrendered my life to Him, I had so much joy on that bed. I don't think I've ever been so happy. I was amazed. *I* did not do that. *God* did, and God gave me a concern for the people there. I was very weak, but I had a little Bible with me, and after a couple of days when I was just a little more stable, I handed it over to the nurse and said, "Would you read me Romans?" So she read me Romans. "Tell me what it means?" I asked. "I don't know what it means," she replied. "What's that word in verse 25 of chapter 4?" I asked further. So she took it home and read the whole book. I did that with her and with several nurses for several days. The weakest possible evangelizing you'd want. But it was bold. I would not have thought it was bold, because it was born out of weakness; but it was also born out of an assurance that I was in God's hands, and the nurses could see that I knew I was in God's hands, and they began to respond to that.

It wasn't long before we had a kind of church down there, with some new converts. We didn't have the sacraments—we weren't there long enough—but amazingly in a Catholic hospital God worked, taking an essentially very, very weak man, then in a very bottomless weakness, and at that point making him bold through the joy of God's presence.

God can use you anywhere. You need to see prayer as precisely what God wants to help you with. If you want the Holy Spirit to become a richer part of your life, you have to stop seeing God as holding back, not liking you because He knows you so well. Rather, you must see that He can't wait to get you to pray, so that He can give you more, so that He can give you the fruit of the Spirit, so that He can cleanse you.

In a revival God begins to make people fit to live with. That's what started the revival in Uganda, and when Joe Church and the Ugandan couldn't get along, they said, "Good night! This is no way for two Christians to live." And they repented, and everyone was so impressed when they saw a missionary and a Ugandan pastor repent. They believed that God was there, and they began to repent too, and a revival went on for fifty years.

I'm asking you to rethink prayer, to see prayer more covenantally, to see witnessing more covenantally, and to see God's commitment in it to you as a son. Out of that, be more daring when you pray. Be more definite, more distinct. Let me give you a short example. In one of my classes, I asked my students to take a three-by-five card, write a prayer promise across the top, one of the main ones about the Holy Spirit, and then write down the five names of people they wanted to see converted. I said, "Get specific." One student did it all wrong. He wrote down the name of a prominent entertainer for his first one. I said, "I didn't mean that kind of thing." What I had in mind was praying for people you know and could witness to. Would you believe that two weeks later the prominent entertainer was converted? I was tempted to say: "Put it back on the card. Keep going, brother." The very heart is praying distinctively.

In evangelism this means you are willing to look like a fool. The reason you don't witness more effectively is that you are afraid of being a fool for Christ's sake. Well, stop being a fool for your own sake; that's the choice. Be a fool for Christ's sake.

A Case in Point

After I'd given some of this material in 1971 and 1972, I decided to listen to what I was saying, and I went out and made a fool of myself. I went to a "Jack Frost Freeze" near Westminster Seminary at about the time when New Life Church was starting a prayer meeting. I couldn't get anyone to go with me, but we had a paid assistant, and I told him he had to go. A wild bunch of teenagers (some fifty of them) were there. We went in, and I made a terrible beginning. I said, "I'm Rev. Miller, and I'm looking for the Pagan Motorcycle Gang." I was, I think, a little bit of a fool for my own sake. I don't think that was the best way to go about it. But it got a lot of attention, and out of that night I was really made a fool of. The worst person out there today is married to my daughter. He became the head of our mission to Uganda. Back then, he was the group leader. He was on heroin. I didn't see him sober for, I think, three months—he was either high or drunk. I said, "Lord, I'm going to stay here until someone gets converted." And I stayed there, and I said, "Lord, I see no one is getting converted; I'm just asking you though, why?" I said, "Lord, I believe, I believe you are going to bring us somebody," and at this point this fellow walked up to me and said, "Are you John Miller?" I said, "Yes, I am." I didn't say that right away; I thought maybe I'd better be careful. But I admitted who I was, and he said, "Do you know I've been calling your house?"

We had prayed for this trip out there; we had prayed for it corporately. He told me later, "Do you know I was the rottenest person out there. There was no greater seducer of young people than myself. But I thought I was basically good. And suddenly I got this feeling, I'm evil. I'm wicked." The police had already told him that. It took him two years to pay off all the things he had stolen, and yet he thought he was good. But when the Spirit convicted him, he had such a tremendous conviction of sin. We gave him the "New Life" booklet, he turned to Christ, and he became as daring as we were. He even went down to the local high school with his Bible.

Wherever you are, you are a son of God. Pray boldly. Act boldly. I want to pray for you in closing.

> Heavenly Father, we really don't know much about praying. We're good at talking. We're good at gossiping. We're not good at praising, and we're not very good at witnessing. We want to be honest, and we want to have You deal with us where we really are. We also have many lusts and ambitions. And we are often fools for our own sakes. But we want to be different. We want to get rid of this. We want to become fools for Christ's sake. We ask You for mercy. We are not talking about someone else; we're talking about ourselves. We need to have Your compassion over us. We ask You to pity us with Your fatherly heart and eye and send Your Spirit to cleanse us and to give us a new joy, a new fellowship with You, a new eye to see that You are our Father, a new glorying in Christ, a new glorying in You, a new freedom in the Spirit, a new setting aside of anxieties, a

deep awareness that there is nothing You are not sovereign over. We pray Father, that You would bring us the comfort of knowing we are wonderfully loved by our God, that we might in wonder and trembling joy take the pardon of our God, the pardon for crimes of deepest dye, a pardon bought with Jesus' blood.

Lord, give us the gift of the Spirit to pray. Revive us, change us, make us different: that we might forgive our enemies, and bless them, that we might love our friends, that we might be tender to those nearest us, that we might be the vehicles of Your ministry in our age. Open our eyes to see evangelistic opportunities. May we have a heart to see, a mind to see; may we love people. May we realize that John 3:16 is applicable wherever we are, that men are under Your wrath and Your curse, but You also offer them a beautiful redemption in Jesus Christ. Redemption brings life and not death. Cause us, then, to proclaim the realities of this new life. Awaken us to the peril of men; help us to see that they are lost, that they are dying without Christ. When they go to hell, that door shuts; it will never be reopened. Lord, give us the knowledge of Your truth. Cause us to live, and then, Lord, as we go forward, daily teach us to pray. Daily teach us to love and to reach out. Now, God, whatever has been helpful from this, take it and cause it to remain, that it might be turned into burning faith and intelligent thinking, that it might be fruitful for many lives. Amen.

_4_

Preaching and Evangelism
Dirk J. Hart

In the New Testament any follower of the Way could preach or declare good news. Luke reports that Jesus said to someone, "Follow me," but the man wanted first to bury his father. Then Jesus said, "Leave the dead to bury their own dead; but as for you, go and proclaim the kingdom of God" (Luke 9:59-60).[1]

Jesus sent the disciples out on a preaching and healing mission (Matt. 10:5; Mark 6:7), and also the seventy. The Gadarene demoniac is told, "Go home to your friends, and tell them how much the Lord has done for you, and how he has had mercy on you" (Mark 5:19). The disciples are charged with preaching the gospel to the whole world (Matt. 16:19; Mark 16:15; Luke 24:47-48; John 20:21; Acts 1:8). Persecuted believers were scattered "and went about preaching the word" (Acts 8:4; cf. 15:35). In order that the apostles could devote themselves "to prayer and to the ministry of the word" seven men were chosen to administer the daily distribution of food (Acts 6:1-6). But at least two of these men turned out to be preachers also (Acts 7; 8:5). The Thessalonian believers "sounded forth" the Word of the Lord everywhere (I Thess. 1:8). All this is summarized in the familiar words of I Peter 2:9, "But you are a chosen race, a royal priesthood, a holy nation, God's own people, that you may declare the wonderful deeds of him who called you out of darkness into his marvelous light."

Today we have a more restricted understanding of preaching: we

---

1. Scripture quotations in this chapter are from the Revised Standard Version.

mean by it the exposition and application of Scripture by an autho-
rized and ordained minister under the supervision of the elders.
Charism has become office. In the New Testament, evangelism,
understood as bringing good news with a view to conversion, was
not a subject to be debated and endlessly defined. It was as natural
as eating and breathing. All of the theology of the New Testament
comes out of the missionary context. As Christ was sent into the
world, so is the church. The question of evangelism never came up.
The heartbeat of the church was in missions and evangelism. In the
intervening years, however, this too changed. There are all kinds of
historical reasons for this, not the least of which is the tremendous
success the church enjoyed until it became the majority faith in
many lands and Constantine established it.

In Reformed theology a distinction has often been made between
missions and evangelism. Missions is considered to be gospel outreach to those who have never heard the gospel or to those who are
far away geographically or culturally. Evangelism is construed to be
gospel outreach to those who have strayed from the covenant and
those who are most like ourselves ethnically and geographically. I
have searched in vain for the origin of this distinction or its biblical
warrant. I know it was widely held by Dutch theologians in the first
half of this century and is still held by *Die Gereformeerde Kerk van Suid
Afrika*. This distinction is useful insofar as it helps us to tailor the
communication of the eternal gospel to the needs, circumstances,
and backgrounds of those to whom we preach. But on the whole the
distinction only confuses a work that is already too much restricted
by distinctions, theological pronouncements, and ecclesiastical inversion. There is only one gospel to be preached. This gospel is the
power of God for salvation to everyone who has faith (Rom. 1:16).

It would be of great benefit to the spiritual health and vitality of
the church if we could let go of some of our officialness, our love of
control by rules and regulations, the theological walls we build
around the gospel, and recapture the New Testament atmosphere
in which preaching and evangelism could be and was the task of all.
We need to read again Roland Allen's *The Spontaneous Expansion of
the Church*. By "spontaneous expansion" he meant, among other
things, "the unexhorted and unorganized activity of individual

members of the church explaining to others the gospel which they have found for themselves."[2] He goes on to say, "Whether we consider our doctrine, or our civilization, or our morals, or our organization, in relation to a spontaneous expansion of the church, we are seized with terror, terror lest spontaneous expansion should lead to disorder."[3] In the church today we need to ask in all serious-ness whether our love for order and control has quenched the Spirit who first came upon the church in a rushing, mighty wind and in due time toppled the temple and built a new temple wherever men and women called upon the name of the Lord.

The Covenantal Context

Keep these things in mind as we turn more specifically to the topic of preaching and evangelism. By preaching I mean the explanation and application of the Word of God, the Bible, as it is addressed to God's people gathered for public worship, usually on Sunday, with a view to the edification of believers. By evangelism I mean this same explanation and application of the Scriptures with a view to the conversion of the uncommitted.

It is important to see the larger context of preaching and evan-gelism. Both are distinctly covenantal activities. God has sover-eignly raised up a covenant people, reconciled them to Himself by His Son, and revealed Himself by the inspired Word. His people are to grow up to maturity and be equipped for ministry (Eph. 4:11-16). The covenant has universal dimensions and intentions. The prom-ises of the covenant are not only to "you and to your children" but also "to all that are far off." God has His elect people everywhere and among all peoples, "everyone whom the Lord our God calls to him" (Acts 2:39). The Great Commission of Matthew 28 is a republi-cation of God's promise to Abraham that "all peoples on earth will be blessed through you" (Gen. 12:3). This was, says the apostle Paul, "the preaching of the gospel beforehand to Abraham" so that all who have faith may claim Abraham as their father (Gal. 3:6-9).

2. Roland Allen, *The Spontaneous Expansion of the Church* (Grand Rapids: Eerd-mans, 1962), p. 7.

3. Ibid., p. 13.

Those who formerly were strangers to the covenant and therefore separated from Christ have "been brought near in the blood of Christ" (Eph. 2:12-13). By His coming, Christ has brought to an end all hostility and division between those of every language, race, and nation who have faith and made them members of one body, the household of God. The message that brings them together is the same for all: "And he came and preached peace to you who were far off and peace to those who were near" (Eph. 2:13-22). Seen from the perspective of the covenant, therefore, preaching and evangelism are inseparably connected.

The Dimension of Worship

Preaching and evangelism also have their own primary context. Preaching is done in the context of public worship of the church, and evangelism is done in the context of the mission of the church, with mission here understood as all that the church is sent to do and say in ministry to the world.

Nothing is more characteristic of God's people than that they worship the triune God from whom all blessings flow. Our entire lives are to be lived as liturgies of love to God in response to Jesus Christ. This is the proper covenantal response to God. When God published the covenant to Abraham, we read, "Then Abraham fell on his face" (Gen. 17:3). This response is further described by Paul when, having lauded the depths of the riches and wisdom and knowledge of God and ascribed to Him glory forever (Rom. 11:33-36), he says, "I appeal to you therefore, brethren, by the mercies of God, to present your bodies as a living sacrifice, holy and acceptable to God, which is your spiritual worship" (Rom. 12:1). Similarly, the apostle Peter urges his readers to be "built into a spiritual house, to be a holy priesthood, to offer spiritual sacrifices acceptable to God through Jesus Christ" (I Pet. 2:5).

The response of worship in the totality of life comes to full expression in the public, corporate worship of the gathered congregation. This public, corporate praise of God has its roots in tabernacle and temple worship and continues for the people of God who are "grateful for a kingdom that cannot be shaken and thus . . . offer to

God acceptable worship with reverence and awe" (Heb. 12:8). The congregation gathered for worship is in many ways the address of the church where it is most at home and at its best.

The greatest sin in worship is to be boring, apathetic, or dull and to be so predictable and safe in the order of events that all sense of expectation is gone and no surprises are possible. Churches that pride themselves in being "nonliturgical" can be so rigid in what may and may not happen in the service that it seems the Holy Spirit must feel straitjacketed by our patterns.

In corporate worship God calls the meeting. He sets Christ on center stage and says, "Let's talk." God's praise is sung. He is adored. The worshipers bring their entire lives and offer them to God. God says, "Grace to you and peace," and the people respond, "Holy, holy, holy, Lord God Almighty! Early in the morning our songs shall rise to Thee." There is intercession and thanksgiving. The high voltage of the Spirit can scarcely be contained in the acts of worship. We adore Him even speechlessly or are struck dumb by our lack of conformity to God's law only to hear anew God's forgiveness through Jesus Christ. There is instruction, encouragement, and consolation from God's Word. There is an intensity about all this that can scarcely be obtained by worship in solitude. God's people are a body with many members. Christ is present in a special way where more than the individual gather for worship (Matt. 18:20). If we embrace God, it is only because He has first embraced us as part of His people and incorporated us, by baptism, into His covenant people. There is, therefore, a primary vertical dimension in worship that gives public worship its unique power. The people respond, and God continues to speak and act.

There is, however, also a strong horizontal bond in public worship. It is after all, corporate worship. The Book of Hebrews emphasizes this when it says, "Let us consider how to stir up one another to love and good works, not neglecting to meet together, as is the habit of some, but encouraging one another, and all the more as you see the Day drawing near" (Heb. 10:24-25). We therefore embrace not only God, but one another: "He who does not love his brother whom he has seen cannot love God whom he has not seen. And this commandment we have from him, that he who loves God should love his brother also" (I John 4:20-21). In the worship service, distinctions of class or kind fall away between those who love God. Otherwise we make distinctions among ourselves "and become judges with evil thoughts" (James 2:1-9). Not only is the worship service "the assembly of the first-born enrolled in heaven," but there is communion there too with "innumerable angels in festal gathering" (Heb. 2:22-23). The cohering reality of it all is in Jesus Christ who is both eldest brother and Lord.

Worship is something we do; we engage in it. Body and soul are stretched; heart and voice are heard. We are not simply spectators but actors. And we bring into worship everything we are as citizens of a heavenly kingdom who are in the world but yet not of it. In public worship the church is to be seen at its best: faith, hope, and love are in full bloom; grace, mercy, and peace shine. There is a seamless robe of fellowship there between sisters, brothers, and their Redeemer, and on the robe are the words "healed and forgiven."

For these reasons worship has tremendous evangelizing power. Many believers today can testify that the first conscious stirring of the Holy Spirit in their lives came as a result of what they felt and observed in a public worship service. The welcome they received, the friendship that was offered, the concrete joy that was present, motivated them, in turn, to listen to what was said and to respond in repentance and faith. Genuine Christian worship demonstrates what cannot be observed and heard anywhere else in the world: Spirit and truth (John 4:24).

The Dimension of Mission

But there is more to this connection between preaching and evangelism. The church of God is an apostolic, missionary people. As Christ was sent into the world, so too His people are sent. The same Spirit who once was given to Christ without measure is now given to His people (John 20:21-22). The covenantal promise that "all peoples of the earth will be blessed through you" (Gen. 12:3) was republished when Jesus said, "you will be my witnesses . . . to the end of the earth" (Acts 1:8).

This essential missionary nature of the church is not something that can be turned off or on. The mission of the church is at the heart of what it means to be God's people. In fact, worship rises from mission, participates in the work of this mission, and leads to mission. God is a missionary, evangelizing God who calls unto Himself a missionary, evangelizing people who worship Him while on their missionary pilgrimage.

Because, as I have said earlier, the address of the church where it may be found at home and at its best is at the gathering of God's people for public worship, the erroneous impression is often left with God's people that the only business of the church is worship and the edification of those who are already believers. About this Paul Hoon in *The Integrity of Worship* writes, "Materials commonly used in worship reinforce this inversion and edify the congregation in a bad rather than in a good sense. Many church rites, prayers, responsive readings, invitations to worship . . . reinforce a congregation's preoccupation with itself."[4] He adds, "An unlearning of the *esse* of the Church as only cultic and *a relearning of the esse of the Church as also apostolic* may need to be the first order of business, and in very practical ways. This may require for one thing a change in strategy whereby the pastor reconceives his priorities, first sensitizes the layman to experiences of ministry in the world, and then works inductively into the meaning of liturgy. And as long as liturgical action is understood as having integrity only insofar as it embraces both, and as long as the presence of Christ is understood as the source of the life and the shape of the mission the layman lives out in the world, such an approach may be indicated."[5]

Preaching Good News

I have set preaching and evangelism in their contexts of worship and mission and asserted that these two essential tasks of the church may not be practiced in isolation from one another. How does this affect week by week preaching? Evangelism is, at its simplest, preaching good news. And preaching good news is the centerpiece

4. Paul Hoon, *The Integrity of Worship* (Nashville: Abingdon, 1971), p. 332.
5. Ibid., pp. 333-34.

in the Reformed worship service. Preachers and books on preaching tend to qualify sermons in many different ways. A preacher may give doctrinal sermons or catechism sermons or a series of sermons on the Apostles' Creed or expository messages on a book of the Bible. He may preach "through the Bible" with one sermon on each of the sixty-six books of the Bible or a series of messages on Old Testament characters. Sermons may be topical or semitopical in nature, such as when the preacher deals with marriage and family life. The great moral problems of our day such as abortion, nuclear armaments, sexual behavior, and materialism may be dealt with. The pulpit cannot and may not ignore the social and political questions that are faced nationally and internationally. But all these sermons will have in common that they are gospel preaching: the good news of Jesus Christ crucified, risen, ruling, and coming again.

Sermons will warn, teach, exhort, comfort, inspire, encourage, motivate, convince, stimulate, lead to decision, and build up the saints—and in doing these things they will always be gospel: the good news of Jesus Christ.

"It is my contention," writes John R. W. Stott, "that all true Christian preaching is expository preaching."[6] The classic Reformed method is to take one or more verses of Scripture, distill the central theme, and then organize the material with several subdivisions. Application may be made throughout the sermon or primarily at its conclusion. Add an introduction, and the sermon is ready to be preached. It must be emphasized, however, that what is preached must not be merely the verse or verses, but the entire Word of God and therefore Jesus Christ. Mere moralizing diminishes our Lord and counterfeits the gospel. Believer and unbeliever alike will be exhorted to trust Jesus Christ as the only way to God.

There is only one gospel—only "one body and one Spirit . . . one hope . . . one Lord, one faith, one baptism, one God and Father, who is above all and through all and in all" (Eph. 4:4-6). There is not one gospel for the world and one for the church; there is not one gospel for the covenant backslider and one for the pagan. As Paul says so graphically to the Galatians, "But even if we, or an angel

6. John R. W. Stott, *Between Two Worlds: The Art of Preaching in the Twentieth Century* (Grand Rapids: Eerdmans, 1982), p. 125.

from heaven, should preach to you a gospel contrary to that which we preached to you, let him be accursed. . . . O foolish Galatians! Who has bewitched you, before whose eyes Jesus Christ was publicly portrayed as crucified?" (Gal. 1:8-9; 3:1).

Unbelievers in the pew must hear this gospel loud and clear. If they do not hear it and go home accursed, it is the church and the preacher who, according to Ezekiel and Paul, have blood on their hands (Ezek. 33:1-9; Acts 20:26-27). Joyful and celebrative as worship must be, varied and broad as preaching may be, they are at the same time a matter of life and death.

Preaching as Teaching

The Scriptures do distinguish in the matter of preaching and teaching between milk and meat. Paul explains to the Corinthians that they are as yet babes in Christ, in need of milk and still not ready for meat (I Cor. 3:1-2). And the writer to the Hebrews wants to go on from elementary and foundational teaching to matters that lead to maturity (Heb. 6:1). I do not propose that the missionary nature of the church and the inevitable evangelistic dimension of preaching demand that sermons always be milk. The people of God do need to be fed the meat of the gospel in order to grow to maturity. I would like to make some observations about this, lest we think that the evangelistic interest of the church will limit the preacher to the ABCs of the gospel.

First, the people of God, believers and their children, gathered for public worship are always a mixture of the spiritually mature, the immature, and the unconverted. Therefore, the milk of the gospel must never be missing.

Second, the spiritually mature who can be fed spiritual meat but who complain when the ABCs of the gospel are proclaimed thereby call into question their maturity. The believer's ear never tires of hearing Christ proclaimed as crucified, risen, ruling, and returning. The call to conversion is applicable to all since we believe that conversion is not only the initial turning to God but equally a lifelong process of sanctification (cf. Heidelberg Catechism, Lord's Day 33). The genuinely mature believer will pray for and expect that in the worship service there will be room for the beginning of faith on the part of the uncommitted. In this connection D. Martyn Lloyd-Jones issues an important warning: "I am urging that all the people who attend a church need to be brought under the power of the gospel. The gospel is not only and merely for the intellect; and if our preaching is always expository and for edification and teaching it will produce church members who are hard and cold and often harsh and self-satisfied. I do not know of anything that is more likely to produce a congregation of Pharisees than just that."[7]

Third, in feeding spiritual meat to the congregation, remember this: meat is best digested in little pieces, one bite at a time. The pulpit is no place for a display of abstract theological learning and a scholar's vocabulary. We must disabuse the congregation of the notion that "deep" is the same as difficult and that "real" Reformed teaching goes over the heads of most people. It is a perpetual challenge for the preacher to preach gospel meat in a simple, transparent way.

Fourth and finally, we need to remember that spiritual maturity comes not only by right learning but also by right practice. Orthodoxy and orthopraxis belong together. I take Ephesians 4:11-16 as teaching that the "measure of the stature of the fulness of Christ" comes at least in part as the saints minister to one another and to the world in word and deed. It is the universal experience of the church, for example, that those members who learn to articulate the faith to their neighbors find this to be a significant means of grace and growth in their own lives.

The relationship between preaching and evangelism demands that the congregation be well instructed in the nature of the church as God's missionary people. This will require preaching on the biblical texts that teach this—a series of sermons on the Book of Acts, for example. It is important to orient the congregation to its evangelistic task and the consequences of this for worship so that pew and pulpit act on the same assumptions and live by the same expectations.

Paradoxically, the relationship between evangelism and preach-

7. D. Martyn Lloyd-Jones, *Preaching and Preachers* (Grand Rapids: Zondervan, 1971), pp. 152-53.

ing also requires a careful balance between what may seem to be self-serving concerns and concern for others. The church does not exist for the world, nor does the world set its agenda. The church exists for God. He sets the agenda. It is God's aim to restore the fallen creation, to set it "free from the bondage to decay" (Rom. 8:21). To that end He sent His Son into the world and gave to the church His Spirit as a guarantee of the full inheritance to come (Eph. 2:13-14). Already all things are under Christ's feet (Eph. 3:22). Until the time comes for the completion of all things when every knee shall bow to God and give Him praise (Phil. 2:11), there is an interim agenda for the church—to acknowledge Christ's universal authority and, therefore, to make disciples of all nations (Matt. 28:18-19). It is a mistake, therefore, for the church to be preoccupied with itself, to be ecclesiocentric. Rather, the church is preoccupied with its Lord and His authority over all things and concern for a new creation. Preaching reflects this and lets the light of the gospel illumine all the various questions, trends, problems, and issues with which the world struggles. It is in the light of the gospel that sin appears at its shabbiest, that the idolatry of our political ideologies is laid bare, that injustices are clearly seen, that our vaunted power structures are exposed as demonic. Jesus is Lord! That confession has consequences for our personal lives as well as all of life. This preaching of Christ's lordship establishes a beachhead in the hearts of individuals—hence even when gospel preaching highlights the cosmic dimension of the kingdom, such preaching must often be accompanied by the demand for personal repentance and faith and the promise of eternal life (Rom. 14:16).

Invitational Preaching

Does the relationship between preaching and evangelism demand an invitation, the so-called altar call? In the Reformed tradition, altar calls of any kind have been avoided. Grace is sovereign and does not depend on emotional manipulation. The entire "invitation system," as it has been called by Iain Murray in a book by that title, rests on an Arminian theology of human autonomy and free will. In some fundamentalist quarters the giving of an altar call is axiomatic—one simply has not preached the gospel without it. In the Reformed churches we need to examine our opposition to this and ask whether our neglecting the invitation is based on a rejection of methodistic and Arminian extremes or on our understanding of the gospel. For all his opposition to the invitation system, Iain Murray says quite rightly, "There is no discussion about whether it is right to invite men to come to Christ. That issue should be indisputable to those who believe Scripture. Nor is it an open question whether man's responsibility to repent and believe should be emphasized in evangelism. Without such an emphasis there can be no evangelism at all in any biblical sense of the word."[8]

The gospel is by nature invitation. Jesus invites and says, "Come" (Matt. 11:28). Because He is Lord, the invitation is also a command. Preachers should not hesitate to stress the invitation and command. The church that takes its evangelistic mandate seriously will from time to time make that demand very specific and indicate how those who are led by the Spirit to respond may make this known and seek further help. It is instructive to read what D. Martyn Lloyd-Jones says about this. After extensively dealing with the error of the altar call, he nevertheless says: "The appeal should be implicit throughout the whole body of the sermon, and in all that you are doing. I would say, without hesitation, that a distinct and separate and special appeal at the end after a break, and after a hymn, should only be made when one is conscious of some overwhelming injunction of the Spirit of God to do so. If I feel that, I do it; but it is only then. And even then the way which I do it is not to ask people to come forward; I just make it known that I am ready to see them at the end of the service or at any other time. Indeed, I believe that the minister should always make an announcement in some shape or form that he is available to talk to anybody who wants to talk to him about their soul and its eternal destiny."[9]

Before I come to the conclusion on the subject, the question arises whether the preacher should exhort people to be diligent witnesses and evangelists in their daily life, work, and relationships. Insofar as this is taught in the Scriptures he should without a doubt do so. But

8. Iain Murray, *The Invitation System* (Carlisle, Pa.: Banner of Truth, 1967), p. 6.
9. Lloyd-Jones, p. 282.

only if the preacher himself is prepared to be a model and to take along one or more members on his evangelistic visitation. If the preacher is not prepared to do this, the congregation will not be either. All preachers should ponder again what Paul says to Timothy: "I charge you in the presence of God and of Christ Jesus who is to judge the living and the dead, and by his appearing and his kingdom: preach the word, be urgent in season and out of season; convince, rebuke, exhort, be unfailing in patience and in teaching. . . . do the work of an evangelist, fulfil your ministry" (II Tim. 4:1-5).

Conclusion

Having examined the relationship of the church and preaching in the light of the missionary nature of God's people, I urge you, let the church open wide its doors and invite and expect people of every kind, class, and color to taste and see that the Lord is good and His mercy extends over all He has made. I am saying this for the good of the church, for its growth, and for Christ's sake, who did not reject the adulterous woman at the well, or the children, or the tax collectors, or any sinner who sought Him out. Indeed, He was not content to wait for them; he sought them out.

I do not at all mean to say that evangelism or evangelistic concerns should somehow take over the worship service. There will always be a sense in which the unbeliever is an outsider looking in. True worship is an act of those whose hearts are made right by faith in Christ. The integrity of worship must not be destroyed by making the service into a gospel crusade rally. But it is precisely the integrity and power of such true worship accompanied by the preaching of God's Word that will lead the inquirer to conversion and to declare, "God is really among you!" (I Cor. 14:25).

All of this has tremendous practical consequences for everything that happens before, during, and after the worship service. We need, in the light of the missionary nature of God's worshiping people, to examine not only preaching but also such things as the welcome extended to members and visitors, the announcements made in the bulletin and service, the prayers, the celebration of the sacraments, and the hymns that are sung.

In Matthew's Gospel there are two occasions on which Christ promises His continued presence—a presence that is at the heart of covenantal life. In the first instance he says, "Where two or three are gathered in my name, there am I in the midst of them" (Matt. 18:20). In the second, Jesus meets His disciples in Galilee following His resurrection. There they worship Him, and Jesus declares to them His authority, commands them to disciple the nations, baptizing and teaching them, and says, "Lo, I am with you always, to the close of the age" (Matt. 28:17-20). Thus Christ joins, with the promise of His presence, these two central tasks of the church: worship and mission.

— 5 —

Evangelism Through Small Groups
Frank M. Barker, Jr.

Throughout the New Testament, the most common setting for evangelism is the small group, very often in someone's home. In this chapter I will focus on evangelism in and through the small group setting because I see it operating not only in the Bible but also in the church I pastor, the Briarwood Presbyterian Church in Birmingham, Alabama. And I see it working in amazing ways in many parts of the world.

Small group evangelism can be conducted in homes, restaurants, offices, hospitals, and almost any place where people gather. For a number of years I led an evangelistic Bible study in a conference room at the Medical Center in Birmingham every Tuesday at noon. Normally we would "brown bag" it, but once each month we had a covered dish luncheon. What a crowd would turn out!

The Purpose of Such Small Groups

Small groups can serve a number of different purposes. One, they promote spiritual growth among those who are Christians. Acts 2:42 says about the early church that "they continued stedfastly in the apostles' doctrine and fellowship, and in breaking of bread, and in prayers" (KJV). These basic elements grow in rich measure in the home Bible study atmosphere. Often I have seen people who had been nominal Christians for a number of years catch fire spiritually when they began attending a small group Bible study.

Two, small groups nurture new Christians. The recent convert needs an environment of intimate support. It is one of the best ways to do follow up. A businessman whom I led to Christ a few years ago was reluctant to become involved in a small group Bible study. It was necessary for me to follow him up individually for several months. Finally he agreed to come to the Bible study for a trial visit. He became so excited about the quality of relationships he found in that group that he started an additional group in his own home the next week. While continuing to come to my group, he worked at inviting his unsaved friends to the new group in his home. He is now an elder in our church and has completed seminary.

Three—the focus of this chapter—small groups provide evangelistic outreach. Small group evangelism can be done in homes and office buildings. It can be targeted toward groups such as students, housewives, and professional people. It can be with friends and relatives. Recently two young mothers whom my wife had led to Christ asked her to speak at a coffee they hosted on "The Real Meaning of Christmas." They invited seventy of their friends and fifty came. At the close of the meeting my wife asked if any might be interested in a small group Bible study. Fifteen responded. She led a study with these women for six months, and the women decided to ask me to conduct a study in the evening for them and their husbands. This resulted in a number of new evangelistic opportunities, and some new small groups were formed.

Using this approach enables congregations to take the gospel where the unchurched people are instead of waiting for the unchurched to come to our worship services. It thrusts Christians into "neutral territory" for evangelism among people who cannot be reached in conventional ways.

I can cite many examples to illustrate the effectiveness of evangelism through small group Bible studies. A lawyer came to Christ through our church and asked me to have lunch with a contractor friend of his who was having marriage problems. The contractor accepted Christ, and we started meeting weekly for lunch and Bible study. The lawyer had another friend, a medical doctor, and he also accepted Christ and joined the study. A businessman in the church heard of the group and came bringing a former employer. After several weeks this man also accepted the gospel. We all prayed for the contractor's marriage, and it was put together. We also helped several men, who had lost their jobs, find new employment, and the group provided support and encouragement in the interim.

How to Start a Small Group Bible Study

Where do the teachers and leaders for such groups come from? Often there are people available in the churches who possess the expertise to lead small groups, and it is simply a matter of recruiting and challenging them. In some cases a training class is helpful. In our church we have a quarterly training class that studies I Peter. Each trainee is given the opportunity to lead the group several times and is made familiar with the various Bible study aids available. Besides being able to lead inductive study, the leaders you appoint must have a real heart for evangelism.

Yet another way of training leaders is to start a group led by the pastor or some other experienced person and let that group be a training ground for other leaders. When the leader has to be away, he or she can have someone from the group fill in. As the gifts and skills of the group members develop, they can be invited to form new groups of their own.

The hosts in the homes where the groups meet are as crucial as the leaders. Hosts need to have the gift of hospitality! People will enjoy coming to their homes, and their hospitality will greatly facilitate the outreach nature of the group.

For a year I lead a group that met in the apartment of a medical student. The student's wife was warm and outgoing, and she continually invited other couples living in the apartment complex. Every Tuesday night the small apartment was jammed, and there were always new faces. The real key to the effectiveness of the group resided in the host couple! Their warmth and friendliness were crucial to the witness and growth of the group.

The hostess of the group I am currently leading is also an excellent example. She always has name tags ready when guests arrive. She phones people who need a little prodding. She prays over each person in the group. She always has extra Bibles available. As an effective hostess, she realizes the importance of tying people together by webs of friendship.

Where do you enlist people to become involved in these groups? There are a variety of approaches. Once you introduce the concept and let it be known that leaders are available, opportunities to organize classes in homes, offices, and restaurants may begin to appear. Or you may approach couples and singles from the church and recruit them to be part of a group for ten to twelve weeks.

You may also preach a message explaining the small group concept and the opportunity for evangelism it presents. Have response cards in the bulletins for people who would like to become involved. In this way you find people to start the groups, and through them you can recruit others.

Another method is to target specific groups such as doctors, dentists, or young business leaders. For example, several years ago some men and I made a list of thirty business leaders whom we then proceeded to invite to a weekly noon Bible study in a downtown office conference room. An oral surgeon in our church followed the same procedure and organized Bible studies for dentists and dental students. Several of our ladies targeted young wives and started a "Mothers and Others" group, which regularly features aspects of homemaking along with evangelistic Bible study. Singles and young career people or retirees can also be targeted; both age groups have proved to be responsive to this approach.

Another way to start groups is to divide a congregation geographically and select a host couple and a teacher for each area. The nucleus of the group in each area should come from the church's membership; this nucleus is challenged to invite non-Christians. For example, each fall we hold Bible studies in twenty to twenty-five geographic areas. Names of church visitors from the various areas are channeled to the host couples, who invite them to join the local group. This approach has proved very effective, and recently six new couples were incorporated into one area Bible study through this referral method.

In order to guarantee that the groups grow evangelistically, it is critically important to build a system of accountability. After recruiting a core of Christians, get them together to pray and plan. Ask each one to give the group the names of several couples or individuals whom he or she plans to invite. The group should pray for these persons, that they will respond to the invitations. After several days it is advisable for the pastor to call all the core people to see if they have invited the individuals on their lists.

How to Conduct a Small Group Bible Study

The hours when studies are held are determined by the members' schedules and circumstances. It's important not to keep people too long. For night groups, I like to start at 7:30 and break up about 9:15. We usually have light refreshments and fellowship from 7:30 to 7:45. This allows time for late-comers to drift in and for newcomers to get acquainted. In some groups we spend some time singing, accompanied by a piano, guitar, or sing-along tape. There is a sharing time of about ten minutes. Then we study the Bible until 9:00 and close with a time of prayer. If we want to go a bit longer, there may be a testimony or two, or small group discussion and prayer. Usually the members stay around for another fifteen minutes of fellowship.

The approach or method used for study can vary considerably. Topical studies on such themes as "Overcoming Depression," "Dealing With Anger," and "Resisting Temptation" are generally popular. Personally, I prefer the inductive approach to studying books of the Bible. When I'm conducting a study based on a New Testament book, I try to cover about half a chapter each night. In a book like Genesis, I generally move faster. In the inductive method, the leader takes the group through the passage following the "observation, interpretation, application" format and using discussion questions. Ideally the leader will also develop the passage in outline form as he proceeds.

It has been my practice to prepare discussion questions for the leaders of our Area Bible Studies series each fall. A sample of these question sheets appears at the end of this chapter. Some of the subjects we have studied are The Epistle to the Colossians, I John, The Sermon on the Mount, Great Interviews With Jesus, Great Moral Issues Facing America, The Book of Job, and Themes From Proverbs.

I have known of some very effective home Bible classes in which the leader used a lecture format, but I prefer the guided discussion.

When a new person comes in after the group has started, he is given a copy of the material we are using and is encouraged to pick up right where we are. On occasion I have used study books such as the *Fisherman's Bible Study Guides* by Harold Shaw. I have also used *Basic Christianity* by John R. Stott and have led the group in a discussion of each chapter. We have used books on marriage and the family as well. Any group leader intending to use a book as a basis for study should be reminded that most group members are reluctant to do homework. Most of what happens will take place during the group meeting.

How to Evangelize in Small Groups

The evangelistic thrust of small group studies takes place in several ways. To begin with, the nucleus of Christians must bring non-Christians into the group. It is not an evangelistic event if the whole group consists of Christians. The recruiting of non-Christians should be an ongoing process so that every week someone new is present.

Each lesson should be complete in itself, even though it is part of a continuing study. The lesson should include content and application for both the non-Christian and the Christian. The atmosphere of the group should be warm and open enough that a non-Christian will dare to ask for clarifications, challenge the leader, or even question what the Bible teaches. The non-Christian should not be put in a position where he feels singled-out, or "buttonholed." In *Lifestyle Evangelism*, Joseph Aldrich lays down some excellent ground rules for evangelistic small group studies:

> First, the purpose of the study is evangelism. Second, the non-Christian must feel comfortable and welcome. Third, most of the discussion should involve non-Christians. As a general rule, the Christian should avoid active participation in discussion. Fourth, religious clichés should be avoided. Fifth, discussion of various churches and denominations should be avoided. Sixth, Christians should resist the temptation to "straighten out" doctrinal views of the participants which are not central to the issue of salvation. The issue is Jesus Christ, not infant

baptism, total immersion, the inspiration of Scripture, pretrib-ulationism, or Post Toasties. Seventh, the Christian should refrain from bringing up all kinds of parallel passages. As a general rule the study should confine itself to one passage. Anyone can make significant observations on five or six verses. However, once the "resident experts" start spouting off other passages, the non-Christian realizes he is outgunned and out of place. Eighth, as a general rule, the Christian participants should avoid giving advice or sharing pious platitudes and spiritual Band-Aids. If they share, it should focus on their personal experience of the truth, not an untested list from some seminar or textbook. Ninth, the Christian must avoid the temptation to press for premature decisions. Tenth, the Christian should avoid the "holy huddle" syndrome. Some of your best friends may be there, but your mission is to reach out in love to the non-Christian. He must be made to feel special. He is!

The gospel should be brought out clearly at some point in each study, remembering that for some in the study this might be the first or the last time they hear it. The evangelistic impact can be heightened by having an individual or couple share a personal testimony at the close of the study.

After each study I try to make an appointment with any non-Christians or newcomers who are there. We go to breakfast or lunch, or I drop by their homes to become better acquainted. Often at that meeting I will go through the gospel using the Evangelism Explosion method or something similar. Usually I find them receptive after they have been exposed to the group study. It is very important that new people not feel pressured and that our evangelistic approach be low key. In some cases the situation may dictate that that first home visit or lunch date be only a friendly get-acquainted time.

As an illustration of how evangelism takes place through a small group study, let me relate what occurred during one of the fall studies I was leading. A church couple brought a neighbor lady to the study. I asked her if I could drop by her home on Saturday to meet her husband and get better acquainted. She agreed and later told her husband. He assured her he would leave to avoid the meeting. However, he didn't leave, and when I called on the home, I was able to direct the conversation to the gospel. It turned out neither was a Christian. She was ready to respond to the message, but he was not, although he listened intently. I urged him to attend the study and he agreed. Before I left the home, I said to him, "If there is the least possibility that what I have said is true, it is the most important thing in the world. And as you have indicated, you haven't really examined the matter. The best way to do that is in a small group Bible study. What about coming this Thursday night?" He came the next week, and he introduced himself to the group by telling us he had committed his life to Christ since our conversation. The man and his wife are now leaders in our fellowship.

Christians involved in small groups have many opportunities to participate actively in evangelism. For one thing, their very presence in the group facilitates evangelism. When they know how to share their faith with others and can give a testimony of God's grace in their lives at the meetings, it makes an impact. Obviously, the more people a church has that are trained in personal evangelism, the more effective any method of outreach is going to be.

Effective evangelism involves relationship building. Christians must be willing to invest time and effort in relating to non-Christians, particularly those whom they bring to the study group. They can discuss the lesson together on the way home or at some later time. They can build relationships through social activities, sports, and other areas of common interest. Christians involved in small groups find they have opportunities for evangelism at many levels, as many in fact as they can handle. The group study approach is basically low key and long range. It is important to avoid pressing for premature decisions, but instead to build solidly through the study of the Word and the interaction of the group.

A very important factor in developing effective outreach is to motivate and teach church members to build bridges to the non-Christians around them. Christians tend to have fewer and fewer non-Christian friends as time goes on. This tendency must be reversed, and Joe Aldrich has made some excellent suggestions as to how it can be done. I will summarize what Aldrich proposes:

1. Visualize the Spirit of God hovering over your neighborhood. Believe God will lead you to people.

2. Make an initial acquaintance with the people in your neighborhood. Block parties, Christmas open houses, and other neighborhood activities provide opportunities for exposure.
3. Establish a growing relationship. Take the initiative to be helpful when it is appropriate. Offer to mow the lawn and look after the house and pets while they're away on vacation. Take their children on a picnic with yours.
4. Extend an invitation to your home.
5. Cultivate common interests such as tennis, golf, fishing, or jogging.
6. Make holidays count. Have a Christmas open house.
7. Be available for those who are hurting. And let others help you when you are in need.
8. Become a giver of books like *Mere Christianity*, material on the family, or a tape.
9. Find an appropriate vehicle for closer contact such as a home Bible study or an evangelistic dinner.
10. Be ready to share the content of Christian faith and your experience of walking with the Lord.

The best way for pastors to teach these principles is to practice them. It is good to conduct a class or seminar on evangelistic methods, but the crucial thing is to model the methods yourself.

Prayer is another vital aspect of evangelistic thrust. The Christian nucleus needs to be praying earnestly for non-Christians in the group and others whom they want to invite. It is important for the nucleus to get together periodically for evaluation and prayer. In one group I led, the host and I would jog together at the "Y" on the day the group was to meet and then sit in his car and pray for the working of God's Spirit that night. I've seldom had a group with such evangelistic thrust!

Aldrich says, "You have not because you phone not." Next to prayer comes phoning. It is my practice to pick up by car several non-Christians or new converts and take them to my class until I feel they are really locked into the group. If I can't pick them up personally, I phone someone to do so on my behalf.

Recommended Literature on Small Group Evangelism

There are many good books on how to begin and operate small

groups. For motivation and insight on the principles and potentials, Paul Yonggi Cho's book, *Successful Home Cell Groups* (Logos, 1981), is the classic. Dr. Cho has built his congregation around such cells. It is the largest in the world and also one of the best shepherded. Every member of the church belongs to a cell group, and there are over 20,000 cell groups in the church. If each cell evangelizes one family of four during the year, 80,000 people are added to the membership of the church. Cho contends that cell group evangelism will work anywhere, but it requires the wholehearted commitment of the pastor. If cell groups are to succeed, says Cho, the pastor must become so convinced of their necessity in the church that he will see them as the key to the life or death of the congregation. Moreover, the pastor must be the primary leader, training the cell leaders and motivating them to reach the goals that have been established for each group.

Cho advises pastors to start small, train some laymen as cell leaders, and have them form their own home cell meetings. Watch over them carefully for six to eight months. Once they are bearing fruit, the pastor can expand the program and involve the whole church. Obviously, the selection of the right leaders at the beginning is crucial.

Cho teaches his people to be alert to the needs of their neighbors. He calls it "holy eavesdropping." For example, a Christian woman overheard another woman say her marriage was in trouble. The Christian woman introduced herself, saying, "I couldn't help overhearing what you said. My marriage was in trouble, too. I'd love the opportunity to share how it got straightened out." As a result the woman and her husband joined a Bible study cell and eventually became Christians.

I have cited the important book by Joseph Aldrich several times. A helpful booklet to use in training people to lead inductive Bible study is *Leading Bible Discussions* by James Nyquist (Inter-Varsity Press). For small group study material, Inter-Varsity has produced a number of study guides on different Bible books. The material published by Neighborhood Bible Studies is good, and Shaw Publishers puts out a series called *The Fisherman's Study Guides*. I have published two booklets designed for group leaders, *The Gospel of John, A Study Guide for Groups* and *I Peter Study Guide*.

How to Develop Close Relationships Within a Group

Various things help to break down barriers and weld a group together. For example, a group can take on a project to help someone. On one occasion the host of a group I was leading suffered a heart attack. He had been planning to paint his house; the group got together on a Saturday and painted his house. It did wonders in welding the group closer together.

One of the men of Briarwood Presbyterian Church holds a weekly Saturday morning Bible study and breakfast at his home. This group has enjoyed a very high degree of closeness and evangelistic thrust. A key to this has been the fact that every two or three months the group goes for a weekend of skiing in the mountains of North Carolina, where the leader owns a cabin, or to Florida for fishing. Sharing picnics, going together to a movie, attending a conference, or going away for a retreat can all contribute to the closeness of a group.

How to Put New Life Into Old Groups

Over time, groups have a tendency to become ingrown. Various methods can inject needed new life. For example, a covered dish supper can be scheduled to which everyone is expected to bring both a dish and a friend. This can help rejuvenate the group, but it will require that the hostess call each wife or single during the week and say, "I am coordinating the food. What are you planning on bringing? And whom will you be bringing?" If no new person has been invited yet, the hostess's response must be, "All right, I'll call you back in an hour and find out whom you're bringing. Remember, you have not because you phone not!"

A special film can be presented on the night of the supper, or you may want to have the usual Bible study. But, whatever it is, it must be particularly adapted for the new folks. I led a group that had about twenty in it, and when there had been no fresh faces for a period, I said, "It's time for a covered dish supper!" The hostess made the phone calls as outlined above and then called me in desperation: "Sixty people are coming!" We moved the study to the backyard, and forty of the sixty indicated that they would like to be part of a regular group. So we split the class and formed a new group.

Films as well as special speakers can be a real drawing card. The Moody Science Films, the James Dobson "Focus on the Family" series, "The Conversion of Colonel Bottomly," "Strike the Original Match," "Chariots of Fire," "Wiretapper" (the story of Jim Vaus), and Chuck Colson's testimony are just a few of the excellent films that can be used in this way.

It is important to maintain a good balance between fellowship, sharing, prayer, study, and testimonies in the group. If the group becomes imbalanced, and this includes the study going too long, it can hurt the group. A Presbyterian pastor, Jim Tozer, who has made excellent use of small groups in his church, insists that the study be conducted around a dining room table with everyone participating. Then they get up and go into the living room for sharing and prayer. He feels the change in location changes the atmosphere and helps bring about the desired results.

How to Get Started

I have given suggestions as to how to train leaders and recruit people for core groups. I suggested starting small until you work out your format and approach, and then starting additional groups. Now comes the question of how a church actually gets started and how Christians phrase the invitation to people they want to bring in.

Joe Aldrich gives some suggestions on how to invite people to come to a Bible study. An invitation may go like this: "I'm sure you are aware, Bill, of the pressures on the family today. Homes are breaking up at an unprecedented rate. Ruth and I are concerned about these trends, and we have invited five or six couples to participate in a study of biblical principles of marriage and family life. We'd love to have you join us." The invitation is sincere, low key, and without pressure. There is honesty about the religious nature of the meeting. The topic is stated clearly and is of common interest.

Aldrich suggests that if the study is going to focus on one of the books of the Bible, an invitation might sound something like this: "I know you are aware of the fact that for years the Bible has been the number-one selling book in the world. No man is really educated who is not at least familiar with its basic content. We thought it would be fun to get seven or eight couples together and work through selected portions of John's Gospel. The study will be informal and discussion-centered. We'd love to have you join us."

The last key I mention is faith. It's the first thing, really, because without it the whole approach fails. The pastor, and after him the church people, must believe that these principles will work and that through their application people will respond to the gospel and Christ will add to His church. As Jesus said, "According to your faith be it unto you."

FALL HOME BIBLE STUDY SERIES

"Great Interviews of Jesus"

WEEK OF (Mon.-Sat.)	STUDY TOPIC	SCRIPTURE
Sept. 12-17	Christ's Interview With a Swinger	John 4:1-42
Sept. 19-24	Christ's Interview With a Wealthy Young Man	Mark 10:17-31
Sept. 26-Oct. 1	Christ's Interview With a Noted Theologian	John 3:1-21
Oct. 3-8	Christ's Interview With a Desperate Mother	Matt. 15:21-28
Oct. 10-15	Christ's Interview With an Inquisitive Bureaucrat	Luke 19:1-10
Oct. 17-22	**Home Missions Speakers—All Tribe Groups Meet on Thursday**	
Oct. 24-29	Christ's Interview With a Destitute Woman	Luke 21:1-4
Oct. 31-Nov. 5	Christ's Interview With a Workaholic	Luke 10:38-42
Nov. 7-12	Christ's Interview With a Troubled Politician	John 18:28-19:6
Nov. 14-19	Christ's Interview With a Terminal Case	Luke 23:39-43
Nov. 21-26	**Do Not Meet—Thanksgiving Week**	
Nov. 28-Dec. 3 Optional	Christ's Interview With a Disciple Turned Skeptic	John 20:24-29
Dec. 5-10 Optional	**Christmas Party**	

DISCUSSION QUESTIONS

For the Week of September 26-October 1

Christ's Interview With a Noted Theologian
John 3:1-21

Read
1. vv. 1-2   What kind of a man was Nicodemus? Why do you suppose he came by night? Why do you think he came at all?

2. vv. 3-7   What is the nature of the new birth? What does the phrase "born of water" mean in your opinion?

3. v. 8   How is the new birth like the wind?

4. vv. 9-13   Nicodemus is slow to understand. How did you respond when you first heard the term "born again"? Can any of you recall your reaction? Why does Jesus upbraid Nicodemus about his slowness? Did the Old Testament teach anything about the new birth? (cf. Ezek. 36:25-27; Jer. 31:31-33). Does anything strike you about Jesus' claims or attitude in these verses?

5. vv. 14-15   Now read Numbers 21:4-9. What points of similarity do you see between the serpent being lifted and Christ's crucifixion? In view of the lifting of the serpent as a type or prediction of Christ's death, why is Christ symbolized by a serpent, the emblem of evil? (cf. II Cor. 5:21).

6. vv. 16-17   What was God's reason for giving His Son? What does it mean to "believe in Jesus"? Can you illustrate the difference between believing "about" and believing "in" Jesus? Is believing in Jesus the only condition of being saved, or is repentance required also? (cf. Luke 13:3; Acts 20:20-21). What is repentance?

7. vv. 18-20   According to these verses, what is the basic reason men don't respond to the gospel? Aren't many kept away by intellectual difficulties? Did you respond to the gospel when you first heard it? Would some of you share what held you back?

8. v. 21   Is Jesus saying that some men by nature "do truth" and respond to light? If men do respond, to what is it due? (cf. I Cor. 2:14; 12:3). Can a person know that he is born again? How?

The leader may want to choose a person or a couple beforehand to give a testimony at the close.

__ 6 __

A Full-Service Church

Bartlett L. Hess

A financial consultant recently came to our church just after he had visited the Calvary Church in Charlotte, North Carolina, Billy Graham's home church. He took a good look at me and said, "You're quite a contrast to Ross Rhodes, the pastor of that church."

"How is that?" I asked him.

"Well, he's six feet four, impressive and intimidating."

"God uses all kinds of different people," I said to him with a smile. I've always belonged to the order of Zacchaeus and have rejoiced that Michelangelo and Napoleon were only five feet tall— shorter than I.

Why did I go into the ministry? Like all other ministers, I had alternative choices. I might have aspired to eminence as a scholar. At age twenty-three I was awarded the Ph.D. degree in modern European history at the University of Kansas. That was fifty years ago. The same day I received Phi Beta Kappa. I have read all sorts of things in my life and enjoy study. But God called me to the pastorate: "Feed my lambs . . . feed my sheep" (John 21:15-17). "Go out into the roads and country lanes and make them come in, so that my house will be full" (Luke 14:23). I started to minister to a congregation at the age of nineteen and have been doing it ever since. I love to preach, and I preach three times every Sunday morning. "Woe to me if I do not preach the gospel!" (I Cor. 9:16) is a theme of my life.

I'm thankful that God called me to serve Him as a Presbyterian. When I moved from a Scottish congregation on the west side of Chicago to a Czech congregation in nearby Cicero, I broadcast a

81

radio program. The minister of the First Christian Reformed Church, who heard the program, called me to say, "I'm glad to see that you are not only evangelical, but also Reformed!" Well, I should hope so! My father, my father-in-law, and I have given over 150 years to pastoring Presbyterian churches, and I'm sure my Reformed convictions can be detected in my messages.

In evangelism, we of the Reformed tradition must come to terms with the question, "Does election cancel out evangelism?" Because some of our ancestors gave the wrong answer, God sent people like Whitefield, Wesley, and others to lead the church back into evangelism. We today must answer the question ourselves, "Does election cancel out evangelism for me?"

In the pioneer days of 1800, three Presbyterian ministers went to the top of Cane Ridge in eastern Kentucky to pray for revival. When they came down, the Cumberland Revival had begun. The Methodists took that revival and ran with it. I heard Bishop Arthur J. Moore say that the circuit riders of the early nineteenth century burned out and on an average died in twelve years. But wherever their saddle bags landed, there a Methodist church sprang up.

In colonial times, Presbyterians outnumbered all other American churches, except in New England, where the Congregationalists held sway. The fire of evangelism never disappeared among us Calvinists, though at times it was dimmed. At the beginning of the twentieth century, churches in the Reformed tradition produced Billy Sunday, J. Wilbur Chapman, and William E. Biederwolf. They also produced multitudes of pastors with hearts of compassion for the lost.

My father was a minister who moved every two years or less. During my growing up period, I attended eight different schools in six states from Massachusetts to Washington. I learned flexibility at a young age—I became used to adapting to new and strange situations. During my last two years of high school, my father ministered to two of the branch churches of the First Presbyterian Church in Seattle, Washington. Mark Matthews, the pastor, had developed thirty branches, all part of the membership that totaled 8,000. This experience, along with observing my father's church planting, gave me the idea that new churches could be started, and once started they should grow. The God whom my father preached about, and by God's grace I too proclaim, is the creator and establisher of the church; and with Him behind it we can expect the church to grow.

God, the Source of Evangelism

The Scriptures make it plain that, in evangelism, God is the source of everything. "All this is from God, who reconciled us to himself through Christ and gave us the ministry of reconciliation" (II Cor. 5:18). "All that the Father gives me will come to me, and whoever comes to me I will never drive away" (John 6:37). "For God so loved the world that he gave his one and only Son, that whoever believes in him shall not perish but have eternal life" (John 3:16). "No one can come to me unless the Father who sent me draws him, and I will raise him up at the last day" (John 6:44). "For he chose us in him before the creation of the world to be holy and blameless in his sight. In love . . ." (Eph. 1:4).

We build the altar as Elijah did on Mount Carmel. Only God can send the fire from heaven. "But you will receive power when the Holy Spirit comes on you; and you will be my witnesses" (Acts 1:8).

Evangelism is a process in and through which God works out His saving purpose. Our Lord told a parable about the mysterious and marvelous power of the seed—planted, germinated, pushing up through the soil. The gospel grows like that. Paul plants, Apollos waters, but God gives the increase. A Sunday school teacher plants a seed, a Christian neighbor bears a humble witness, an evangelistic service causes the person to come under conviction, and a membership class brings him or her to definite decision. Many human agents are involved, but all through the process God works to accomplish His saving purpose. Billy Graham expressed it well some years ago when he was preaching in Nairobi, Kenya. Thousands filled the stadium, and on the side sat a row of missionaries, some of them veterans of many years in Africa. Graham gestured to the missionaries and said, "You planted the seed; I am reaping, and God produces the harvest."

The Evangelism Process at Ward Church

At Ward Church we receive an average of 400 new members each year. Thirty percent of them come on profession of faith. I am often asked, "How do you do it? What draws so many people to Ward Church?"

Let me explain first of all that as the pastor of Ward Church, I do not feel that I myself possess the special gift of evangelism. Not every pastor has that gift, though each one is responsible for the work of evangelism in and through the church. When Paul wrote to Timothy and commanded, "Do the work of an evangelist" (II Tim. 4:5), he prescribed something that all of us commissioned to give pastoral leadership should do. At the same time I admit that though I have led many people to Christ in my private office and in the pulpit through the exposition of Scripture, I do not consider myself as having the special gift of evangelism.

What, then, does a pastor like me do in order to organize and implement evangelism in the church? After careful analysis of myself and my ministry, I realized that I had to find a method that fitted my gifts and abilities. As the pastor and teacher of Ward Church, I had the responsibility to lead in evangelism, and I had to discover and use the method that was effective for me. I found it through the teaching and discipling process that has proved to be a hallmark of Ward Church. Membership classes have proved to be an ideal way for me to cast the net, and we've seen hundreds of conversions through these classes and the whole system developed around them. God promised to honor His Word taught and proclaimed, and we see the promise fulfilled over and over again at Ward Church.

People come to Ward Church for many different reasons. Only God knows how He motivates them to turn in our direction. But here I will explain the process we employ; I hope it will give you and your church some helpful ideas:

1. *Location.* The church stands on a corner, almost in the center of the suburban community of Livonia, Michigan, an upper-middle-class suburb of Detroit. I chose the location carefully after consultation with church planting experts. It is easy to

locate, with plenty of parking, and the whole community is aware of its presence.

2. *Variety of Programs.* We minister to the community through our community Bible class, youth programs, singles' ministries, and educational opportunities for all ages.

3. *Public Relations.* People we do not even know recommend our church. A Roman Catholic said to a new neighbor who moved in, "Are you Protestant? If we were Protestant, we would go to that Ward Church."

4. *Witness and Invitation of Ward Members.* Our members are great at sharing the gospel, and they enthusiastically recommend our church as they move around in the Detroit metropolitan area.

5. *Momentum.* People may first come out of curiosity to see what draws people to a crowded church and parking lot. What happens after the first visit depends on the quality of our church and ministry.

6. *Meeting Needs.* At Ward Church, we constantly seek to identify people's needs and meet them. People hear that the "food" is good, and people's needs are met. When they discover for themselves that this is true, the flow keeps moving in our direction.

7. *Media Coverage.* Radio, television, and newspapers have featured special ministries of our church such as Single Pointe. The *Detroit News* carried an article about the financial growth of our church when other churches were hurting.

8. *Active Publicity.* At Ward, we publicize. We do not hide our light under a bushel. Some people drive from as far away as thirty miles to attend Ward Church, and this is largely due to our aggressive publicity efforts throughout the metropolitan area.

What happens when a person or family comes to our church? Each signs his name on the ritual of friendship, which is passed down the row. In the next few days, I—or one of our telephoners, evangelism volunteers, or staff—call them up. Were they just visiting for the day? If so, I thank them for coming and do not follow up. Are they new in the community or looking for a church home? Or are they spiritually hungry, perhaps not born again? If so, we put the name or names on our list of prospects, and that sets wheels turning.

By careful assignment, new prospects are called on by organized callers on Tuesday night, or by members who live near their homes. Prospects are invited to a class or small group for growth and cultivation. Family members are followed up by persons their own age or by staff members responsible for that age group. Prospects will be invited to a newcomers' dinner where music, singing, testimonies, and information about the church are shared.

Cell Organization

Ward Church has 170 cells, with a deacon in charge of each cell. Our goal is to integrate the evangelistic thrust into this cell organization. One person in each cell is responsible for cultivating prospective members in his or her cell's area and incorporating the newcomer into the cell.

We hold membership classes for adults three times each year—fall, winter, and spring. New people are invited to sign up for these classes with the assurance that they may attend classes without committing themselves to join the church. The classes consist of nine weekly sessions. Each session consists of a thirty-to-forty-minute lecture, followed by small group discussion. The leaders are well trained in teaching and group dynamics. Participants receive printed outlines of each lesson and guidelines for the small group discussion. The topics covered during the first four sessions are very basic: God, the Bible, the nature of man, Jesus Christ, God's way of salvation, the sacraments, the church. These sessions lay the groundwork for a responsible decision about the Christian faith.

At the fifth session, those attending are given an opportunity to sign up for church membership. This involves signing a profession of faith in Jesus Christ as Savior. Not all sign. Those who do, continue for three more sessions. At the seventh session each person is interviewed for fifteen minutes by several elders, who seek to make sure that each person understands the statement of faith he or she has signed. If the elders are not sure, a pastor deals with the individual further. At the eighth session, those wanting to join are transferred to the Minister of Discipleship. He discusses the steward-ship of money, time, and talents. At the ninth session, the Minister of Discipleship gives a test to each prospective member for the purpose of identifying each one's spiritual gifts and possible areas of service in the church.

Finally, after a reception at which each member of the church staff describes his role in the church's program, the group of newcomers joins Ward Church. The joining ceremony takes place at a com-munion worship service. It is alway a time of great excitement for the congregation as a whole, and invariably still more people feel the desire to begin the process toward church membership.

The work with new members can't stop here, however, or serious repercussions may occur. We have discovered that after all the weeks of intensive instruction and cultivation, new members get a feeling of letdown unless the assimilation process continues. Our responsibility, therefore, must continue for some time. We must follow up until each new member is thoroughly integrated into the church. For this we depend heavily on the cell organization. We have found that assimilation occurs most readily through the small cell group, for in that circle strong Christian ties are established.

The Growth Environment at Ward Church

Parents know that a baby must be fed, nurtured, protected, given a good environment, loved, cooed over, and surrounded by mature sufficiency in his or her helplessness. Frequently we ignore that same need among new Christians in the church. We give people the rush, get them into the church, and then say in effect, "Make it the best you can." At Ward Church, we have found that if new people do not find their place in three months, they leave us. New members need a cell unit, a Sunday school class or a Bible study group. I think the text that sheds the most light is this: "Like newborn babies, crave pure spiritual milk, so that by it you may grow up in your salvation, now that you have tasted that the Lord is good" (I Pet. 2:2-3). New members need to join the choir, teach a class, usher, work in the kitchen, join the evangelism group, or become a telephoner. Or they must find some other of the myriad opportunities we provide in the church, so that each one may "grow in the grace and knowledge of our Lord and Savior Jesus Christ" (II Pet. 3:18). Nobody stands still. New church members move forward or backward.

Modeling the "Go" of the Gospel

Someone has said that churches can be divided into two kinds: the "you all come" and the "let's all go." The churches that "go" are the churches that win sinners, build them into fruitful saints, and grow large in the process.

When you look at the Scriptures, you see the heavy emphasis on "going" with the gospel. The pastor has to recognize this and model it. "Come and see . . . then go . . . and tell" (Matt. 28:6). "Go into all the world and preach the good news to all creation" (Mark 16:15). "Go and make disciples of all nations" (Matt. 28:19). "Go out to the roads and country lanes and make them come in, so that my house will be full" (Luke 14:23).

George Muller not only fed orphans on faith, but he served at the same time as pastor of a large church. He said, "A home-going pastor makes a church-going congregation." I know that sounds old-fashioned. But early in my ministry I learned an important lesson from a minister in Chicago who said, "When I see a stranger in the congregation on Sunday morning, I try to arrive on his doorstep by Monday night." I took that as advice from the Lord for me, and throughout most of my ministry I went out calling regularly two or three evenings each week.

For forty-five years I have called on new people, unchurched people, trying to interest them in God's message, the church, and active involvement in the Christian life. In the early years of my ministry, when I was pastoring in a rental neighborhood in Chicago, I learned that if you want to reach apartment dwellers, you have to climb the *back* stairs. I climbed the back stairs and then rang the back doorbells in the apartment buildings because people in those places didn't respond to front doorbells.

What did I do once I had reached them and gotten into their homes? First, I did a lot of listening. Where did they come from? What, if any, had been their previous church affiliation? How had they served in their former churches? In one way or another I found out if they knew the Lord Jesus as their personal Savior. I did not press the point too much at first because I did not want to lose the fish before I had hooked him. I always found out about their children, their names and ages, and any special needs they might have. (Children frequently decide where a family will go to church.) Right away I made plans to get the family related to classes, church organizations, and groups congenial to them. I did my best to diagnose what had to be done to prepare them to know Christ as Savior and Lord in the fellowship of our church.

Besides personal calling, I have learned the importance of using the telephone to advantage. I call absentees and sick members and pray with them on the phone. I call new people—and we have 100 to 150 first-timers every Sunday morning—and follow up by telephone on prospects that need further cultivation.

Making the Church Glow

I think it was G. Campbell Morgan who first described a certain ecclesiastical body as "faultily faultless, icily regular, splendidly null." "Dead orthodoxy" is the more familiar expression. Plenty of churches that preach the gospel do not grow. "Many are cold and a few are frozen." We Presbyterians stand for order, but that shouldn't mean rigidity. Legality does not necessitate legalism. Whether in the Pharisees of Jesus' time or in rigid church people of today, legalism kills the spirit. "The letter kills, but the Spirit gives life" (I Cor. 3:6). Legalism quickly darkens the glow of any church.

Love among believers, on the other hand, makes a church glow and attracts outsiders. If you want to create a glow in your church, beware of majoring in minors. Do not make important what the Bible does not make important. And maintain an atmosphere of acceptance that sees each person who comes your way as having been sent by God, needing your ministry and worthy of care and attention.

There is a glow to a church where all kinds of people, of all social classes, are accepted as those for whom the Lord Jesus died. At Ward Church we get all kinds of people. We have the largest singles group, religious or secular, in the entire Detroit area. When we began the singles group, I know what some of the people came for. They were looking for one-night stands, and I could detect it in their eyes. There's not much of that anymore, and we have seen many who came for the wrong reasons born again in Jesus Christ, their lives changed, and their lifestyles forever turned around.

The glow comes through exalting spiritual gifts. Unless the Holy Spirit energizes our ministry and distributes divine gifts, we falter and fail. We learn about this in Scripture passages such as Romans 12, I Corinthians 12 and 14, Ephesians 4, and I Peter 4. God has gifted every believer. It's up to us to recognize and use the gifts He bestows. It's the clue to the glow of a church.

I shall never forget what I heard E. Stanley Jones say when I was a graduate student at the University of Kansas: "We are half-full vessels trying to run over." The stress, the strain, the burnout, come from trying to appear more spiritual than we are, trying to do God's work in man's way, in the energy of the flesh instead of in the power of the Spirit. "If a man is thirsty, let him come to me and drink. Whoever believes in me, as the Scripture has said, streams of living water will flow from within him. By this he meant the Spirit" (John 7:37-39). Sometimes our lives are characterized by undertow rather than overflow. "I no longer live, but Christ lives in me" (Gal. 2:20).

The spirit of the church makes all the difference in the world in attracting outsiders. The presence of the Holy Spirit gives light and warmth. A family who came to our church reported that their little girls said afterwards, "Let's go back to that happy church next Sunday." You can have fellowship without sacrificing worship. I shrink from having everyone stand up in the middle of the morning service and shake hands with those nearby. To me that procedure interrupts worship. Yet we use the ritual of friendship, a book signed by each person in the pew, then passed back so each can see the names. We ask people to introduce themselves after the service to those sitting next to them. Many will bring their neighbors to me and say, "Pastor, these people have come to our church for the first time. Their names are . . ."

Strangers know whether you love people or only pretend to love them and want to use them. No one likes to be treated as a soul to be captured and added like a scalp to a belt. He doesn't want to be viewed only as a member to swell the rolls, or a worker to fill some vacancy. He knows when he's looked at in terms of the dollars he can give. Genuine love for the Lord and for people shines through all a church does. The magnet of love draws people.

Practical Methods That Make a Difference

I'm not averse to discussing methods of evangelism and church growth. Most of the ones I've used are old, while others are a bit innovative. They are as follows:

Preaching

"Preach the Word" (II Tim. 4:2), says the Bible. I preached expository sermons throughout my entire ministry. I have preached through many parts of the Old Testament and most of the New Testament verse by verse. I aim to serve the food on different levels, for different stages of Christian maturity, as well as appeal to the unsaved.

Teaching the Bible

I regard the Bible as God's inerrant Word, and this conviction forms a strategy. Ward Church teaches the Bible in twenty adult classes paralleling the three services Sunday morning at 8:30, 10:00, and 11:30. A psychologist who has a master's degree in biblical studies teaches a class of 600-700. We have a large singles class of several hundred; large and small Bible study classes; classes for couples of different age groups; a young adult class for those of college age, another for those in their twenties, each of these two classes numbering 100 to 200 in attendance. The Sunday school numbers approximately 2600 each Sunday.

My wife Margaret has written a Bible course, which she teaches to between 500 and 600 people on Tuesday morning. She teaches another class in Christ Church Cranbrook in the northern suburbs. Besides this, some fifty to sixty home Bible studies meet during the week; many smaller groups meet to study and pray.

Midweek meetings have proved to be a problem for many evangelical churches across the country. At Ward we have found the solution in a dinner held each Wednesday at church. More than 500 attend, and this frees members from preparing a meal at home and brings the entire family together at church for the midweek classes. We hold eight adult classes besides classes for children and young people. About 1200 are enrolled in Ward's school of Christian education.

Interest Groups

Many of our special interest groups were suggested and started by members of the congregation. Cancer patients meet in "I Can Cope." An alcoholic suggested "Alcoholics for Christ" to take addicts beyond Alcoholics Anonymous. They and their spouses fill several rooms on Thursday nights. "New Dimensions" has attracted many women and some men to study the Bible while they reduce their weight. We have just started a fellowship for those in the medical and health fields to deal with such questions as involvement in abortion or when to "pull the plug." The women's missionary fellowship sponsors craft days. Bowling, baseball, volleyball, Christian Service Brigade, Pioneer Girls, father-and-son canoe trips, dinners, men's prayer breakfasts, finance seminars, a permanent employment committee to help those out of work, a special bulletin board for personal needs for jobs and housing, golf leagues, tennis, teen ski club, teen choir and trips, missionary trips to different parts of the world, a Sunday school class for the mentally handicapped: all of these were dreamed up and are carried on by members of the congregation.

Caring Groups

"The Ward Community of Care, We Care Because He Cares." Christian Love in Action takes meals to people alone, infirm, or having terminal illnesses. The Telephone Listening Center operates twenty-four hours a day in a rented office to listen to hurting people of all kinds and to give Christian counsel. Our 170 deacons each look after ten or twelve families, call on the sick and hospitalized, and minister to those in need in the congregation. Last year the deacons gave out more than $100,000 for rent, heat, food certificates, and camp and college scholarships. Three pastors, an executive committee of ten, seventeen parish leaders, and 170 deacons care for the 170 cells and various ministries of the church.

"Keenagers"

A group for those beyond fifty holds meetings and takes trips to various places such as Williamsburg, New England in the fall, and local attractions. They have occasional luncheons and assist in the office with letters, in the media center, and in many other ways. Some retirees come in every day to help.

Youth

Our youth programs include Sunday school classes, intensive Bible study groups, assisting in vacation Bible schools for city missions and churches, mission tours, extensive trips, popular meetings on such subjects as rock music, choir tours, and drama.

Music

Ward's music department is extensive. There are graded choirs, with 200 members in the chancel choir singing at three services, youth choirs, an orchestra, and bell choirs. Besides these, ample opportunity is given for special ensembles, soloists, and musical events.

Single Pointe

Ward Church offers a divorce recovery program consisting of seven sessions held three times each year, with about 200 in attendance each time. Single Pointe holds a Bible class on Sunday, Talk-It-Over sessions, counseling, mass meetings twice a month on Friday, weekend retreats for all groups, missionary trips, and Bible study groups.

Evangelism Ministries

Tuesday night calling and evangelistic Bible studies form the backbone of this department. There is also the training of the entire congregation in how to share the faith with family, neighbors, and friends and invite others to Ward Church.

World Missions and Church Planting

Last year, Ward Church gave over $700,000 to missions. We support about 140 missionaries and agencies throughout the world. A scholarship fund contributes to the education of our sixty young people preparing for Christian vocation. An older couple has gone to Taiwan to work in a school for missionaries' children. A single, male teacher is serving as a traveling teacher, first in Africa, and now in the Philippines. Our members of all ages have served for shorter or longer periods of time in the Far East, Africa, South America, and Alaska. Retirees and others assist in the work of the church locally and internationally.

Ward Church has started two daughter churches: Trinity of Plymouth, six years old now and numbering over 500, and Grace Chapel, two years old, with more than 250 in attendance. Grace Chapel was organized as a congregation in January, 1985. It has supported itself from the start with a nucleus from Ward Church. We plan to start another church in Brighton, thirty miles to the west, and will continue to organize churches throughout the eighties if the Lord wills.

Ward Church's Building Plans

Our church suffers from what church growth specialists call "sociological strangulation." We have overgrown our site. We cram too many people into too small a space. Eight acres will not hold 5,000 to 6,000 people at one time. We bus our teenagers to another school for Sunday morning classes, and we bus from three locations to our church. We fill every available space of parking on three corners besides our own.

With remarkable guidance of the Holy Spirit, we have purchased 136 acres for $3,050,000, two and one-half miles directly west of our location, a short distance from a major expressway. This will open all kinds of possibilities, not only for parking, but also for evangelizing a community college of ten thousand students down the street from our location and perhaps for building a Christian school and high school, apartments for senior citizens, a youth center, a singles' center, adequate Christian education areas, and staff offices.

When I started my ministry, I never expected it to become so extensive. I give all the credit to God. At each step of the way, I merely tried to pastor my flock faithfully and do the work of an evangelist, as the Lord showed me at the time. Just as when Paul planted and Apollos watered, God gave the increase (I Cor. 3:6).

__ 7 __

Learning How to Witness
D. James Kennedy

Although the program of training laymen for the task of evangelism at the Coral Ridge Church in Fort Lauderdale, Florida, grew out of the specific problems and situation of that church, it contains some readily transferable techniques that have been and can be used by other congregations. We believe that the principles contained in the program represent some of the basic principles of the New Testament concerning evangelism, though by no means does this program exhaust all of the biblical teaching and possibilities of evangelism. It should be stated here at the outset that this is a program of personal lay evangelism and does not begin to encompass many of the other sound and biblical methods of evangelism, such as mass evangelism and pulpit evangelism.

Realizing that laymen are perhaps the most strategic and yet unused key to the evangelization of the world, we have endeavored to build a program that will motivate, recruit, and train men and women to do the job of evangelism, and then keep them doing it. This, of course, is not an easy task, as most pastors can testify. And yet it would seem that the basic principles of New Testament evangelism require this mobilization of the laity. Let us look for a minute at some of these principles.

Examining the Principles

Christ's first instructions to His new followers in Mark 1:17 were, "Come ye after me, and I will make you to become fishers of men"

(KJV). His last words on this earth to His disciples were, "But ye shall receive power, after that the Holy Ghost is come upon you: and ye shall be witnesses unto me both in Jerusalem, and in all Judaea, and in Samaria, and unto the uttermost part of the earth" (Acts 1:8, KJV). Christ thus began and ended His ministry with the command to be witnesses and fishers of men. This thrust of His teaching is summed up in the Great Commission where Jesus commands His followers to go into all of the world and preach the gospel to every creature. The first and obvious principle then is that *the Church is a body under orders by Christ to share the gospel with the whole world.*

But the question then arises, *How is this to be done and by whom?* We believe that one of the greatest victories Satan has ever scored against the church is the idea he has foisted off on probably 90 percent of the Christian church, that it is the task of ministers and evangelists only to share the gospel of Christ and that this is not the job of laymen. So successful has Satan been with this stratagem that an estimated 95 percent of our church members never lead anyone to Christ. Thus the army of Christ has been more than decimated, and the response from the pew has been "let clerical George do it." I am thankful that today there is an obvious trend in the opposite direction, as more and more laymen and churches are realizing and accepting their responsibility to witness. The second important principle then is that *laymen as well as ministers must be trained to evangelize.* Over 99 percent of the church is made up of laymen. Therefore, if they are A.W.O.L., there is little doubt but that the battle will be lost.

The witness of the entire early Christian church produced a tremendous impact upon the world. In Acts 8:4 we read, "Therefore they that were scattered abroad went every where preaching the word" (KJV). But some have said: "Does not this refer to the apostles? After all, what do laymen know about such things?" A standard exegetical axiom is that "a text without a context is a pretext." Thus, this text has been ripped from its context and used as a pretext for idleness on the part of multitudes of laymen. But let us examine its context. In Acts 8:1 we read, "They were all scattered abroad . . . except the apostles" (KJV). Therefore, according to the emphasis of this passage, *those who went everywhere preaching the Word were every-*

one except the apostles. And the term translated "preaching the Word" is from the Greek verb *euaggelizomai,* which means, of course, *to evangelize.* Thus, in the early church all of the laymen went everywhere "evangelizing." This is the lost ideal we are striving to regain.

We have seen what needs to be done and by whom; now let us ask, *How are we going to get them to do it?*

Hundreds of thousands of messages have been preached on the responsibility of Christians to witness, and yet any formidable army of lay witnesses is strikingly absent. Something, therefore, must be missing. This brings us to our next important principle, namely, *"Evangelism is more caught than taught."* This oft-repeated cliché rather accurately describes what is missing in most attempts at teaching laymen to evangelize and also fairly well describes the method Christ used to teach His followers. I have asked thousands of ministers how many of them have preached sermons on the need to witness and have taught classes on this subject. Most of them have raised their hands, but when I have asked how many of them make a habit of taking their people with them when they go out to evangelize, only 3 or 4 percent usually respond. Just this week I questioned a group of ministers, missionaries, and teachers, and found that only about 1.5 percent of their members were regularly engaged in leading people to Christ. Then I discovered that only three of these people took their laymen with them when they went to evangelize. The average person can no more learn to evangelize in a classroom than he can learn to fly an airplane in the living room. The missing link of modern evangelistic training, which was so thoroughly provided by Christ, is *"on-the-job training."*

These most basic principles need to be understood and accepted if a church is to have an effective program of evangelism.

Reviewing the History

This program grew out of the experiences I had in starting the Coral Ridge church, which was a Home Mission project. I came directly to this work from seminary, and though I preached evangelistically and though I had taken all of the courses offered at seminary on the subject of evangelism and read many books besides, I found that the sophisticated people of Fort Lauderdale did not respond to my message from the pulpit. I was totally lacking in both confidence and know-how as far as confronting individuals face to face with the gospel was concerned. After eight or ten months of preaching, the congregation had gone from forty-five to seventeen people, and I was a most discouraged young minister. About this time I was invited to Decatur, Georgia, to preach ten days of evangelistic services. Happy to get away for a while from my Fort Lauderdale fiasco, I accepted the invitation. When I arrived the pastor told me that I would be preaching each night, but more important, he said, we would be visiting in the homes each day—morning, noon, and night—to present the gospel to people individually. I was petrified, for I knew that I had no ability whatsoever to do this. However, the next morning we went out. After about a half-hour of my stumbling attempts at evangelism, the pastor took over the conversation and in about fifteen or twenty minutes led the man to Christ. I was astonished but did not realize even then the impact this was to have on my life. For ten days I watched this pastor lead one person after another to Christ for a total of fifty-four individuals during those ten days. I went back to Fort Lauderdale a new man and began to do just what I had seen done. People responded. Soon dozens, scores, and then hundreds accepted Christ. This principle of *"on-the-job training"* had been applied to my life and had produced its results.

I then realized that there was a definite limit to the number of people that I myself could see, and that what I ought to do was to train others to do the same thing. What I then foolishly did is the same thing that thousands of others no doubt have done: I organized a class on witnessing. I gave them six lessons and sent them out. They all went home terrified! I waited a few months and tried again. This time I gave them twelve lessons—again no success. A few more months and another series, more elaborate, more complex; fifteen weeks—again no results. I do not know of one single adult that was brought to Christ by one of these laymen as a result of these witnessing classes.

Finally it struck me like a bolt of lightning—I had had classes for three years and had not learned how to witness. It was not until someone who knew how had taken me out into people's homes that I finally got the confidence to do it myself. Thus I began the program that has continued for the past six years. It began by my taking out one individual until he had confidence to witness to others, and then another, and another. And so it has grown. After people are trained, they in turn can train others.

Motivating the Christians

Often a pastor will begin an evangelism program by preaching on the subject and then inviting everybody who is willing to take part to come on some specified night. We tried at first to motivate people and recruit them this way but found it was not very successful. The basic motivation will no doubt begin from the pulpit with sermons on the responsibility, privilege, and necessity of witnessing for Christ. The great texts already mentioned, and others, should certainly be preached with clarity and forcefulness. However, our experience taught us that the actual recruiting should not be done from the pulpit, but rather should be done on an individual, person-to-person basis.

Recruiting the Workers

When Christ called His apostles, He first prayed all night and then called them specifically by name. An apostle (*apostolos*) was one sent forth with a commission. The term has both a narrow and a wider meaning. In its narrow sense it refers only to the twelve apostles whom Christ first called. In its broader sense it refers to every Christian who has been sent forth by Christ with a Great Commission. I would therefore recommend that after much prayer the minister select several people whom he would like to take with him to learn how to evangelize. (We have changed from going out two by two to going out by threes because it solved the problem of what to do about women in a program of this sort. To send out two women at night in a large modern city can be quite dangerous; to send out one woman with somebody else's husband can be dangerous in a different way; to send out only husbands and wives defeats the purpose of multiplication.)

We have selected Wednesday morning from 9:00 to 12:00 and Thursday evening from 7:15 to 10:30 as our time of visitation. In each case we have a report-back meeting, which is important to prevent discouragement. On Wednesday noon we have lunch; we provide the coffee, and the people bring bag lunches. On Thursday night we provide Sanka and doughnuts. At these times we hear the reports of the work of the day. These report sessions help reduce drop-outs resulting from discouragement, as workers have their spirits lifted by hearing others whom God has blessed that night or morning. I would suggest then that the pastor select two people for Wednesday and two others for Thursday night. As long as we do not have three men together, which seems a bit heavy, we have not found that the three individuals constitute much of a problem.

We have two training programs a year, the first beginning early in October and running about four and a half months until the middle of February. At this time we hold our week-long clinic for ministers. Then we begin our next training class, which runs until the beginning of summer. Again all of these details will vary according to local customs and circumstances.

I did not want to begin a program in this small way with only one or two individuals, but wished rather to train a whole class of evangelists at one time. The result was that I ended up with none. However, if you begin with a few, you can grow in a short time into a large body of witnesses. At the end of the four-and-a-half-month training program each of these four trained individuals recruits two more workers, and the minister also recruits four more. Now the original four plus their eight make twelve, plus the minister's new four, making sixteen plus the minister, for a total of seventeen. After the next class the sixteen laymen would get thirty-two more, making forty-eight, plus the minister's four, which makes fifty-two, plus the minister, making fifty-three. And soon it could grow to a hundred, two hundred, etc. The people are recruited by personal visits, at which time the program is explained by the trained individual in detail, and then they are invited to a dinner where they hear a greater explanation of the goals and principles and reasons for the program, plus testimonies of what has been accomplished. Then they are asked to commit themselves to the entire four-and-a-half-month training program *or else not to start.* Paul said, "I am afraid of you, lest I have bestowed on you labor in vain."

Training the Evangelists

Our program consists of *three types of training:*

1. *Class Instruction.* These classes are held once a week on the day the people come to the church for visitation. They meet together for class instruction for a half-hour and then go out into the field. During this class instruction there is a brief lecture on the topic of the week, assignments are given for study during the following week, and the class is divided into two's where they practice what has been learned during the previous week.

2. *Homework Assignments.* We have prepared a detailed notebook containing instructions in how to present the gospel logically and interestingly. Assignments to learn portions of the gospel are given each week and are checked and recited each week at the class.

3. *On-the-Job Training.* The third and most important part of the training is the "on-the-job training." Here each trainee goes out with a trained individual and listens as this trained person endeavors to lead someone to Christ. *This is the vital, almost indispensable, element of training.*

Presenting the Gospel

Our basic approach is not apologetic, defensive, or negative. It is a simple, positive statement of the *good news of the gospel.* We have found that most Christians do not know how to make an intelligible, forceful, and interesting presentation of the gospel. This is basically what we try to teach them to do.

We feel that a very useful tool often omitted from texts on evangelism is an actual presentation of the gospel itself. The training materials include such a presentation, and the people are encouraged to learn it and use it as a guide to present the gospel of Christ. Later it is no doubt adapted to the individual personalities with many additions or subtractions made as the case may require. But most people need something to start with.

The essential things we try to teach our people are how to get into the gospel and find out where the person is spiritually, how to present the gospel itself, and how to bring the person to a commitment to Jesus Christ at the conclusion.

In teaching the trainees the presentation of the gospel itself we proceed in the following manner. First, we have them learn the *Outline* of the gospel, which might be considered as the *skeleton*. Second, we have them learn *Scripture verses*, which give *muscle*, so to speak, to the outline. *Third*, we have them learn *illustrations* which *flesh-out* and make clear and understandable the outline of the gospel.

In having the trainees learn the gospel, we do not have them memorize the entire presentation but rather have them first learn the outline and then gradually *build on to it*. First we have them add just enough so that the bones of the outline don't rattle. Then we have them give a three-minute presentation of the gospel. And then we enlarge it to five minutes and then to eight. We continue to enlarge the presentation until they are able to present the gospel in anywhere from one minute to one hour, depending on what the particular situation warrants. We provide them with the long presentation of the gospel as well as a shorter one to use as resource materials from which they can build their presentation on the basic outline. In this way it becomes *their own*. We encourage them to work on it, practice it, give it, until indeed *they own it* and can give it with authority.

Preserving the Fruit

Such a program of evangelism generates a tremendous need for *follow-up*. It has produced a need for a follow-up secretary and also a follow-up minister on our staff, but the main responsibility for follow-up rests with the individual who has led the person to Christ. In our training notebook we have a rather elaborate section on follow-up principles and procedures. In essence the follow-up procedure involves several individual return visits wherein the new convert is established in the Scriptures and assured of his salvation. We use a variety of materials and recommend highly the Navigator follow-up materials. After several personal visits we then endeavor to get them into a small Bible study group which consists of several more mature Christians plus four or five newer Christians. These classes of six or eight people then provide the *spiritual incubator* in which the newborn babe will live out the first few months of his Christian life.

Follow-up procedures are not completed until the convert has been taught to study God's Word, to pray, to live the Christian life, and to walk with Christ. Then he is encouraged to come into the evangelism program to learn how to win others to Christ. Yet at this point the follow-up still is not complete, for he must be taught not only *how to reproduce* but also *how to disciple* his new convert until he has matured to the place where he also is able to bring someone else to Christ. This emphasis on *spiritual multiplication,* looking past the first generation to the second, third, and fourth, is the secret of an expanding and multiplying evangelistic ministry. In just a few years this has produced instances of great-great-great-great-great-great-great grandchildren in the faith. The acid test of any follow-up procedure will ultimately be, *Is it producing spiritual grandchildren and great grandchildren? If not, then something is amiss, and somewhere the process is breaking down.*

Multiplying the Results

Christ said, "The field is the world." I believe that *our field should be the world;* that every church, every individual, has a worldwide responsibility. I do not believe that any church can settle for anything less than worldwide evangelism as its own responsibility. Is it utterly unrealistic? I think not. Eleven men, indeed a very small church, have succeeded in carrying the gospel to most every nation on the earth. And the march of those eleven men goes on today. I do not believe, however, that it necessarily must take hundreds or thousands of years for the impact of the gospel to spread around the world. *The process of spiritual multiplication can grow with the rapidity of the physical population explosion that we are seeing today.* Our goal then is to reach the world for Christ.

How can this be done? First we must realize that *our responsibility extends beyond Coral Ridge or Fort Lauderdale, or even Florida, or the United States.* But how are we to meet this responsibility? We have proceeded in this manner: In addition to training an increasing number of people in our own church (in our last class we had 298 individuals), we have also provided training for a good many other churches in the city and the immediate area. In addition to this we have an annual clinic in February in which we bring down almost a hundred ministers for five days of intensive training, both class-room instruction and on-the-job training, going out with our trained laymen. This has proved very successful, and hundreds of ministers have gone back to their churches with a new vision for evangelism and a new zeal for training their people to do the work of ministry.

There are now churches all over the United States that are build-ing programs of lay evangelism as a result of these clinics. But this does not yet meet the need. After these ministers have trained their people to become evangelists, *we encourage them to have their own clinics,* inviting ministers of other churches to come and learn from their people. These new ministers then go back and train their members, and even hold their own clinics and invite other minis-ters, so that the multiplication procedure continues.

Our first daughter clinic was held with forty ministers in a church in Michigan. A second and third clinic are planned, and so the process continues. This program has already jumped the boundaries of the United States, and such programs are being conducted in a number of other nations. As this is being written, the program is being introduced in Japan. We hope that in the not too distant future there will be churches in every nation that will see the vision of training their laymen and then bringing in other ministers and teaching them to train their people, until a vast army of tens of millions of Christian lay evangelists has been raised up. *This is our goal.* This is our challenge. And by the continual supply of the Spirit of Christ we trust it will be done.

Soli Deo Gloria.

— 8 —

Evangelism Through Sunday Schools
Kennedy Smartt

Through the years most professions of faith in American churches have come through the Sunday school. Yet, when evangelistic strategy is discussed in many Reformed and Presbyterian churches, the importance of the Sunday school is commonly overlooked. Sunday schools are not automatically evangelistic. It takes wise planning, good training, and skillful implementation to make Sunday schools evangelistically effective. In this chapter, I want to discuss the church's use of the Sunday school for evangelization. I hope that churches in the Reformed tradition will learn from this and will make greater use of this effective asset.

My Own Experience

My eyes were opened to the potential of the Sunday school when I pastored a church while in college. The only preparation I had for the job was a three-year stint in the infantry during World War II, which had just come to an end. I had gone to Sunday school almost every Sunday of my life until I went into military service, and I had had several teachers along the way who were concerned that we pupils truly knew Christ as Savior. But not one of them seemed to have a vision for the unchurched people in the neighborhood. Sunday school, it seemed, was for church members and their children. When I began my first pastorate, I had no idea of how to use the Sunday school evangelistically. Not only that, there seemed to be no one who could teach me.

But I had to do something. The church was dying and could afford to pay me only $25.00 per month. (This meant $10.00 for preaching and $15.00 for janitoring.) What does a fellow do in a situation like that? I began to make some discoveries. I found that many more people came to Sunday school when I went to their homes and invited them. I found that when I reached one in a family I often could use that bridge to reach others, sometimes the whole family. I also found that when a person visited our Sunday school, he or she was much more receptive to the gospel when I made a follow-up visit to the home. Finally, I found that growth in the Sunday school inevitably resulted in the growth of the church. New Christians brought their friends to Sunday school, some of them stayed for church, they heard the gospel call, and some were saved. It worked like a spiral, and it was exciting.

You may not believe this, but no one had ever told me such things could happen through the Sunday school. I learned it only when I saw it happen. I discovered for myself that the more I visited, the more people came to Sunday school, the more people were receptive to the gospel, and the more people were saved. And the new converts brought their friends. This was a revelation! I had not seen it in my home church as a boy; no pastor or elder had ever pointed me in this direction. And no teacher of evangelism had ever whispered it in my ear. I had to discover for myself the basic lesson that visitation in the homes of the unsaved and unchurched results in the growth of the body of Christ.

At the time that I started my visitation ministry, quite honestly, I did it out of desperation. I did it because if I didn't do something fast, the church would be gone and I would be left without a job. It didn't occur to me that I ought to be out there pounding on doors because Jesus came to seek and to save the lost, and that has a lot of implications for the church and what it does. I went out seeking people because it seemed the last thing I could try, and in the process God taught me enormous lessons.

I spent three years in that pastorate during my college days and still look back on that experience as a very important part of my education. I learned how to do door-to-door evangelism, build a Sunday school, conduct an evangelistic vacation Bible school,

organize an evangelistic youth club, and use community improve-
ment, employer-employee relations, and social welfare evangelistically. The time was immediately following World War II. The
industrial war machine had come to a halt, and the servicemen had
returned home. Many were unemployed and uncertain about
where to go and what to do. The times provided a tremendous
opportunity for evangelism and an abundance of prospects for
visitation, day and night. Our little church organized a health association and hired a nurse to do home health care. The funds came
from the profits of a newspaper route on the nearby college campus,
where a student in each dormitory delivered the papers and col-
lected from each student, gratis. Baseball and basketball leagues
were organized among a dozen churches in the area, and men and
boys were kept busy. God was gracious, and many people came to
Christ and the church. The Sunday school was bursting at the
seams.

Following those three years I went to a very fine Bible-believing,
evangelical, independent seminary for two years. During that time I
heard nothing about the things I had learned during the three
previous years. The seminary did not intentionally avoid the practical side of evangelism and church growth. But the emphasis was
on academic subjects, as it had always been. Furthermore, there
were no professors in the school who had had extensive pastoral or
evangelistic experience. My own brief pastorate while at college put
me miles ahead of most of my teachers. World War II had marked a
radical shift in many areas, and one of them was from the purely
academic to a more practical emphasis in theological studies. But the
seminary I attended apparently had not heard about the change.

I transferred to a denominational seminary, and again I accepted
the pastorate of a small, struggling congregation located only a few
miles from the school. I was warned that the local denominational
leaders had already discussed the possibility of closing the church. It
was losing members and not attracting industrial workers living in
the area. The church was located between an industrial community
and a metropolitan "bedroom community" composed of middle-
class white collar workers. The church had tried to reach both blue
and white collar communities, but had succeeded in reaching nei-

ther. It was located closer to the industrial community. As for attendance, there were less than twenty-five children and young people attending Sunday school, and the number was decreasing. Obviously it was a church in deep trouble.

But remembering what I had learned in the previous pastorate, I began in June visiting door-to-door from morning until dark. I concentrated on getting to know the young people. In August our vacation Bible school attracted 320 children. Fortunately, the weather permitted us to have most of our classes out of doors, and we were able to use teenagers to teach the little children. We played games, sang a lot of songs, memorized Bible verses, and drank an ocean of Kool-Aid. And the children found out where the Presbyterian church was, and many of the junior and senior high people came to Christ. It was the first time many had ever been inside a church. They became members of our Sunday school and, in time, of the church. Many of their parents were reached also, and the church was on its way to becoming a strong, vibrant, evangelistic center in the community.

Later I was to find out about all the things I was "doing wrong." But by then it was too late. I learned in time that I didn't have to do it all myself, and that it is better for the pastor to train others to visit, evangelize, pray, build bridges, and disciple new converts. In those early days I assumed the pastor was supposed to do it all. But God had His reasons for letting me start out that way, because now as I train others I can teach them the lessons I learned myself in the trenches. Since those days I have learned a great deal about curriculum, organization, vision, goal setting, training, transportation, and a host of other things. But as I look back I wonder what it would have been like if I had learned these things first. Probably, I would have missed the best lesson of all, that evangelism begins with, and never ceases to be, "seeking the lost." As I look back on those days I still feel those door-to-door visits were the most exciting, educational, and productive times of my entire ministry. I was going to seminary at the time and found ample opportunity to put into practice everything I learned in theology. What a privilege!

Are Our Sunday Schools Healthy?

In the decade of the sixties it was being said that the tide was going out on the Sunday school and some were predicting its demise. But the grand old institution has rallied to make all her detractors look foolish. True, Sunday schools with a humanistic base and liberal, man-centered curriculum have withered and died. But thousands of Sunday schools that are characterized by evangelistic fervor, love for the lost, commitment to the Bible as the inerrant Word of God, and the desire to make the Scriptures relevant to people's needs are robust and growing. The exciting truth is that the last half of the twentieth century is seeing an unprecedented number of Sunday schools growing to great size and vitality. This is cause for great rejoicing, and also for great soul searching. Because not all Sunday schools, not even in orthodox, evangelical churches, are healthy and growing. We have to ask the hard question, therefore, as to why some Sunday schools in Bible-believing churches are not doing well, and some are dying along with their churches. The answer is that very basic and important lessons have not been learned.

The Value of the Sunday School

Probably no denomination has concentrated on growth through the Sunday school more than the Southern Baptists. To ignore the lessons they have to teach us is folly. Their two basic textbooks for the Sunday school are *Basic Sunday School Work* and *The Growth Spiral,* and they are available at any Southern Baptist bookstore. There are many more excellent titles available, not only for the Sunday school as a whole but also for each department. There are resource books for planning, growth, curricula, outreach, follow-up, reaching the unreached ethnics, and others. I recommend that every pastor visit a Southern Baptist bookstore and purchase materials. I am thankful that our Southern Baptist brothers and sisters are glad to share what God has taught them.

The Southern Baptists extol the value of the Sunday school in many ways. They call it the largest army of trained workers in the church, larger than church boards and larger than any group trained for evangelism. The Sunday school is composed entirely of volunteer workers who make this their primary ministry in the church and are not burdened with too many other jobs.

Alas, many of us have not learned those lessons! Our Sunday school workers are the same ones who sing in the choir, lead the youth, serve as officers of the church and the women's organizations, and do the visitation evangelism and a host of other jobs we shove onto them.

In most churches, 15 percent of the members are doing 90 percent of the work. This is especially alarming when viewed in the light of studies that show that people remain faithful to a church to the degree that they feel needed and are involved in a significant ministry.

The Sunday school provides a wider range of opportunities for significant ministry than any other area of church work. Many different people are needed—teachers, assistant teachers, officers, outreach workers, and organizers as well as trainers for all these roles. People who feel responsible for a Sunday school activity are much more likely to invite and bring others to the Sunday school and work to make the program grow.

A tremendous asset of the Sunday school as an agent of evangelism is its "open doors" policy. Anyone can belong to Sunday school, whereas only baptized believers can belong to the church. An atheist, agnostic, Buddhist, cultist, or a person living in gross sin can join a Sunday school class. The Sunday school is a hospital for sinners. But how many churches think that way?

Unfortunately the Sunday school in most churches is managed by and designed to serve the "select of the elect," the spiritual elite of the church. It doesn't even reach the peripheral members of the church, much less the "publicans and sinners" of the world. The curriculum is aimed at the mature Christian, as are the program, language, application, and cultural setting. "A hospital for sinners" and an evangelistic outreach into the community are the furthest things from the minds of the leadership of the church when planning for Sunday school.

As I write I am thinking of two pictures. In one, all mankind is divided into two groups, one inside and the other outside a circle. Christ is inside the circle and everyone with Him is a Christian. The circle that encloses them cuts everyone else out. The other picture I have in mind shows Christ at the center, and all others are related to Him like the spokes of the wheel to the hub. Some are deeply committed Christians and they are near Him. Others are growing in their faith and drawing closer; still others may be drifting away, or have not yet begun to stir in response to His love. But the only lines in this picture are the lines that link individuals to Christ. The lines isolate no one. This is the picture of evangelism, the picture in which no one, short of eternity, is cut off.

I believe this second picture is vital to the concept of an evangelistic Sunday school. No one is considered "cut out." Some have already established their linkage to Christ by faith, and their link actually makes their neighbors closer to Christ because the believers represent the presence of the living, loving Christ to them. And the Sunday school, in a sense, offers an opportunity for "belonging" to that person who is not yet a baptized believer. The Sunday school, when viewed evangelistically, represents not the safe harbor of salvation, but a kind of Coast Guard cutter risking the waves to rescue helpless seamen from sinking ships. It is tragic that many Sunday schools have missed, or perhaps consciously refused to adopt, this evangelistic stance toward the unsaved in the community. When Sunday schools are designed and maintained only for the "insiders," we must not be surprised when they make no evangelistic contribution to the church.

For a Sunday school to grow, the senior minister and his staff have to be committed to it. They have to commit themselves to work on it, promote it, plan for it, staff it, and persevere with it. Unfortunately, most ministers today have never been a part of an evangelistic Sunday school and so are not convinced of its value. Many don't even consider it an important part of the life and ministry of the church. They resent its claim on the time and the energy of the layman, and when they see that it is sick, they do nothing to restore it to health. They fail to realize that they are crippling their strongest ally in outreach.

Seven Keys to a Growing Sunday School

Years ago a pastor accepted a call to a congregation in a southern town in which there was a textile community. The families of the men who worked in the textile factories lived in "company houses," and few of them went to church or to Sunday school. The new pastor in town visited these families, invited them to church, and brought them to Sunday school. This had never happened before, and the congregation was not prepared for it. The regular members did not want their children associating with the children "from across the tracks." The officers of the church ordered the new minister not to invite or bring anyone from "the mill hill" again. The minister's reply was to remind his officers that this was the church of the Lord Jesus Christ who said, "Suffer the little children to come unto me and forbid them not." He further stated that he would obey God rather than men. The sad end of the matter was that in a very short time the pastor was out of a job and seeking another church. He was committed to growth, but his people were not. Growth requires the commitment of both. The wise pastor knows he must enlist his people's support before he begins to reach out. That is the first key.

In the example I shared earlier about the church I served while in seminary, we had such a sudden influx of new people that I was fortunate to have a group of officers who were totally supportive. I didn't have sense enough back then to know how important it was to teach and prepare the congregation for the kind of growth God may send its way. But, as a lady once told me, God looks after "children, fools, and Presbyterian preachers." To this day I am not sure which category she put me into. But I am forever grateful for the church officers who even used their cars each Sunday morning to make one or two trips into the working class area where there were children who lacked transportation. Without the help of this committed group I could never have succeeded.

The second key to a growing Sunday school is that we must know the people we are seeking to reach. Few prospects are found accidentally. Perhaps I should say that few prospects come seeking the Sunday school. In our endeavor to reach the industrial community, we did door-to-door visitation, mailings, and telephone callings. We aimed at our target and scored.

Some Sunday schools may find their target community in a new subdivision, a ghetto, or an unreached neighborhood. But most often the best evangelistic prospects are the relatives, neighbors, friends, and associates of existing members of the Sunday school. The secret of growth is to get the members to recognize this, to pray for their unchurched friends and relatives, invite them, and bring them. All the while they must so live and share Christ's love that the people will want to come.

The third key to a growing Sunday school is the creation of an environment in which newcomers will feel welcomed, loved, and important. What visitors perceive as friendliness is the primary reason they return. A friendly climate cannot occur in a situation where people are suspicious, angry, jealous, or opposed to what the church is doing. It cannot happen when some in the congregation are secretly hoping the Sunday school will fail so they can say, "I told you so." But a climate of friendliness is found in a Sunday school and church where the morale is high and the people are pulling together toward common goals. People who are enthusiastic about what God is doing in their lives, and in their church and Sunday school, will communicate enthusiasm to others. They will bring their friends, they will advertise the church by word of mouth (the best kind of advertising), and they will do everything necessary to create a feeling of warmth and excitement. Nothing will keep a Sunday school growing more than that. And nothing will kill it more than dull, joyless, lifeless, thoughtless, unfriendly people.

The fourth key has to do with the quality of the Sunday school staff. A Sunday school will grow where the workers commit themselves to excellence in teaching, visiting, praying, seeking, and winning. Workers who are recruited on the basis of, "Oh, there's really not much to it," will have no respect for the job, and they'll probably do poorly in it. Those recruited on the basis of the high challenge and responsibility involved, coupled with the spiritual rewards of "taking men for Christ," will probably produce a growing Sunday school.

Committed workers deserve good training—the best that is possible and available. To recruit Sunday school workers without providing the needed training is a travesty. Training in how to visit homes, share the faith, and disciple new believers is as important as the "how to" of teaching. Effective training classes in all these areas are the fifth key to growing Sunday schools.

The sixth key deals with building facilities. A church that wants a growing Sunday school will need to plan facilities for it. The highly committed will put up with crowded classrooms, but not the average newcomer, especially if he or she is not a Christian. He doesn't like to stand in line, and he doesn't like to be "packed in like sardines." Rarely does a church put its primary emphasis on building for the Sunday school, but the ones that do are usually growing churches. A second worship service in the morning generally works well to handle overflow attendance. But Sunday schools work best when all classes meet at the same time. Churches, therefore, must plan ahead for Sunday school expansion. To ignore the need for increased building facilities is to put a ceiling on your growth.

I am often asked what can be done when the facilities are just not available. In a case like that we can sometimes turn a weakness into a strength. For example, I taught a boys' Sunday school class early in my ministry when absolutely the only place inside to meet was in the coal bin. That could have destroyed the class, but we billed it as "the class in a coal bin—the only one like it in town." The boys decided this sounded like fun, something to talk about, and they got other boys to come just so they could say they had been to a Sunday school in a coal bin.

The seventh and most important key is prayer. A growing Sunday school needs persistent, prevailing prayer for teachers and pupils, especially those pupils who need to be won to Christ as Savior and Lord. This prayer needs to be coordinated and accountable. It needs to be energized by the Holy Spirit and prompted by a deep love for the souls of persons who apart from the saving grace of Christ will be forever lost.

What do I mean by "coordinated and accountable" prayer? I believe that the answer is one of the most important things I have written about in this chapter. Christ promised in Matthew 18:19, "If two of you on earth agree about anything you ask for, it will be done for you by my Father in heaven." On the basis of that promise, I maintain not only that Christians should have the names of lost friends, relatives, and neighbors on their prayer lists, but also that they should have another Christian agreeing with them in their prayers. It gives us another promise of Christ to claim as we pray, and it makes it a lot harder to stop praying when we know that someone else is also praying for our friends.

I suggest that every Christian start by having a prayer list of his or her own. Then let him or her share a few of the names off that list with one to five other Christians who reciprocate. Let them pray for each other, and for each other's friends in their private prayers and when they meet together. They should pray also for grace to build bridges of friendship and share the gospel. This kind of prayer is "coordinated" and "accountable," and it is hard to give up.

Hindrances to Sunday School Growth

Probably the first and greatest hindrance to growth is apathy, and the cure for apathy has to begin with the pastor. If the pastor is apathetic, the church officers tend to let things slide, and the congregation loses its vision as well. The reason so many churches aren't growing is that no one is holding before them the vision of a world dying without Christ, of men and women, boys and girls, whom He came to seek and save.

More than anyone else, the pastor is responsible for infecting his people with a dream of reaching the lost. It has to be his passion. He has to be the example and the inspiration. He has to find the way to lead his people in such a way that they will *want* to follow. It will mean rising early for prayer and keeping late night vigils for the souls of men. But it can and must be done.

The second hindrance to growth is the lack of necessity. When new members are needed to help pay the pastor's salary, make the mortgage payments, and do all the countless tasks church life produces, then the pastor and congregation work hard to bring in new people. But when the period of urgent necessity is past, the zeal to reach and bring in new members seems to wane. It is sad to admit, but one reason why some churches don't grow is the lack of the feeling of necessity. And I would think that the remedy is obvious to every thoughtful and biblically instructed believer.

A third hindrance is the lack of purpose. All too many Sunday schools have no other purpose or goal but just "to meet." They've always done it a certain way, and it never occurs to anyone to ask "Why?" In order for the Sunday school to play an evangelistic role effectively, it needs to have a clearly stated evangelistic purpose spelled out and agreed upon by the leadership. Once this is done, everything the Sunday school does must be measured by the yardstick of this statement of purpose. Make evangelism central in your statement of purpose, and then work out your purpose. And you'll see your church and Sunday school grow.

A fourth hindrance to an evangelistic, growing Sunday school is the absence of pastoral support and leadership. It is difficult for a football team to score without the quarterback's inspiration and leadership, and this applies just as much to the Sunday school and pastoral leadership. The pastor is only one part of the team, but he is the most important part. He keeps the team moving, he calls the plays, and he watches the goal. Pastor, you must accept your responsibility in this regard. Don't expect anyone else to take your place.

The fifth and last hindrance I will mention is the power of tradition and unwillingness of people to change. Most Sunday schools are not evangelistic and never have been, and it will mean a lot of change to turn them into effective outreach agents of the church. Change means new ideas, procedures, assignments, training, and workers. People, we all know, are creatures of habit, customs, and tradition. "We've always done it this way," is probably heard more often in churches than anywhere else. But to reach unreached children, youth, and adults through Sunday schools means that church members have to accept a totally new concept of who comes to Sunday school, how they get there, what they are taught, and who does the teaching. It may sound radical, and it surely won't be easy, but I guarantee it will be worth the effort.

In conclusion, I suggest that you slant everything your Sunday school does toward growth. Always keep the newcomers and visitors in mind. Plan a curriculum that deals with practical biblical topics that people are concerned about. It is wise to have several adult classes dealing with topics attractive to newcomers. Have regulars in these classes who know how to make visitors feel welcome and can be depended on to make follow-up visits and phone calls. People have a tendency to return when they are made to feel wanted and important.

Most people enjoy fellowship and activities. Each class should have someone planning regular social gatherings, cookouts, picnics, family fun, retreats, excursions, ice and roller skating parties, bowling, miniature golf, and whatever people in your area enjoy. If the facilities are available, a good intramural program of volleyball, basketball, and softball can be a real drawing card. Plan your program to induce growth.

Evangelism through the Sunday school takes work, dedication, persistent and coordinated prayer, and a warm, caring involvement in the lives of others. But the end is to seek the lost and draw them to Christ. Think what this could mean for your church. It can happen if the pastor believes in it, inspires others, provides leadership, and communicates the right goals to the congregation. And then the congregation must dream it too, plan for it, work for it, and pray it through.

— 9 —

Follow-up to Fellowship
James C. Bland III

In evangelism today it is the general rule, not the exception, that workers consider the job done when the person says he trusts Christ for salvation. That is the common attitude whether evangelism takes place in one's living room or at a mass rally in an auditorium. And it is a mistake. The work of making disciples, to which the Great Commission calls us, is a continual process; it must move from initial decision to incorporation into the body, and the key element is proper follow-up. The follow-up pattern of evangelism is written clearly across the face of the entire New Testament. The apostles preached the gospel to the unsaved, gathered the believers and inquirers into groups for further study, and incorporated converts into assemblies of God called churches. They followed up with visits, instruction, fellowship, and pastoral care.

Wherever this pattern is adhered to today, evangelism is an ongoing process leading to incorporation and assimilation in Christ's church. Take for example the case of Bill and Susan Moore.

The Moores attended Grace Church for several weeks and were visited by an evangelistic team. Their hearts, having been prepared by God's Spirit, joyfully received the good news, and they believed in the Lord Jesus Christ. After the Moores prayed and received Christ, the evangelism team spent time reviewing the meaning of their commitment to Christ and the privileges of the new believer. A time was established for a return visit in a few days in order to study a Bible lesson together and to encourage them to attend a small fellowship group the next week. The evangelism team knew that their next objective after the Moores became believers was to begin the process of making them active disciples. From the relationships established in the small group fellowship, the next step was for them to identify with the community of faith by membership in Grace Church. The Moores did in fact find love and acceptance in the small group, and eventually they became a part of the growing fellowship of Grace Church. Each has been given a ministry and has developed a keen sense of being needed. Today they are joyfully growing in their faith in Christ, and they are sharing it with their friends, whom they believe will soon become disciples of Christ like themselves.

The process of follow-up, illustrated by the case of Bill and Susan Moore, does not end, not even when new believers become members of the church. The process continues until the new members are assimilated into the fellowship of the church and are participating in its ministry to others. This is the concept of disciple-making that I want to discuss in this chapter, a concept that is very vital to effective pastoral evangelism.

Immediate Follow-up

A new believer in Jesus Christ needs to be instructed in certain truths at once. First, he needs to know that as a believer he can be confident of salvation. Faith in Jesus is sufficient unto eternal life (I John 5:13). The promises of God in the Bible are enough to affirm this truth clearly, and the Spirit of God within the believer will deepen the conviction as the new life unfolds. At this point it is important that the new believer begin to read the Bible in order to deepen the roots of his faith. The Gospel of John is very useful at this stage, and by reading at least one chapter a day and underlining the words *receive* and *believe,* the new believer will be strengthened in the conviction that he has in fact received the gift of eternal life by believing in the name of the Lord Jesus.

Second, the new believer must be encouraged to converse regularly with God through prayer. Through Jesus Christ the Mediator, he can talk to his heavenly Father and bring Him his cares and needs as well as the praises of his heart.

Third, the new believer must be made aware immediately that God is to be worshiped, not in isolation, but in fellowship with others. He may be a long way from understanding this yet, but the truth must be planted in his mind and heart. One of the persons involved in the evangelistic ministry should invite the new believer to church the next Sunday and should pick him up so that they can go together.

Just before the immediate follow-up is concluded, another visit or appointment should be scheduled. It should be within the next seven days. In the meantime, at least one phone call is advisable, preferably within twenty-four hours of the initial visit. By phone the evangelist can ask if there are any questions that the new believer may be struggling with, and he can encourage the person to remain firm in his commitment to trust God completely for forgiveness and salvation and to pray for growth in faith and the Christian life.

First Week Follow-up

The objective of this next visit is to solidify the new believer's commitment to the Lord Jesus Christ and to encourage his growth in grace. Ideally the visit should be conducted in the home of the new believer. By this time he should have read the third chapter of John. The evangelist briefly tells the story of Nicodemus and underscores the truth of being born again. The new believer is reminded that Christianity means a personal relationship with God and leads to growing fellowship with other believers. After the new convert has attended church with the evangelist, he should be encouraged to join a small fellowship group.

First Month Follow-up

Christ's command is to make disciples. Therefore, the evangelist's responsibility has just begun once the person is headed in the right direction. The discipler has the primary responsibility to see that the new babe in Christ continues to grow. During the next contact, perhaps on the way to the small fellowship group, the importance of regularity in public worship should be explained along with the truths of personal Bible study and prayer. The evangelist should encourage the new disciple to verbalize his new faith to others, and this is obviously a major step, for now his life must become a witness to what he believes.

Incorporation Into the Visible Church

After successfully proceeding through the initial steps, the new believer should identify with the church. The importance of this step must be stressed in our day because many who profess to be Christians do not see the value of church membership. A recent Gallup poll disclosed that Americans are praying more and reading the Bible more, but they are not attending church as often!

The church is the family of God, the covenant community, and God calls believers to identify themselves publicly with His people. Church membership is a serious step, and the new believer must be guided and prepared to take the step intelligently and with commitment.

Assimilation Into the Fellowship

Even incorporation into the visible church does not end the evangelist's responsibility. The new believer must be assimilated into the fellowship of Christ's visible church, or else there is a strong chance that he may slip away. Many newcomers are lost to the church because members involved in evangelism quit too soon. They assume the task is over when the new believer has been introduced to the church and made a few friends. But when actual assimilation does not occur, or is somehow aborted, the new person drifts away, and there is painful disappointment on all sides.

It should be noted that this kind of slippage occurs less often when believers are introduced to a small group fellowship very early in their development. Those who are not involved in small group life are the ones most vulnerable, and they often slip away within a year. If new members don't find the love and acceptance they are looking for, they may decide to look for it elsewhere.

The word assimilation is not in the Bible, but it certainly conveys a biblical truth. It touches the very essence of the church, which is a covenant community composed of people in fellowship with God and with one another. The entire Bible is the story of God's coming to fallen man redemptively and by grace calling out a people that assembles to worship Him and disperses to serve Him.

We discover the meaning of assimilation in the Greek word for fellowship, *koinonia*. *Koinonia* means more than merely an association of people. It means "shared life." The model of the shared life for the New Testament church was the fellowship and ministry of Jesus with His disciples. When the disciples became apostles and fanned out across the Roman world planting churches, they carried with them the model of a shared life, the *koinonia* of believers in Jesus who lived daily in shared fellowship with God and with one another.

Koinonia leads to *diakonia*, service to the Lord and to others. The body of Christ joined together and gifted by the Spirit for service becomes God's instrument to carry out His purpose in the world.

During the time of the Great Awakening, John Wesley organized his followers into "class meetings." His method was criticized, but Wesley knew what he was doing. He wrote, "Many now happily experience that Christian fellowship which they had not so much as an idea before. They have begun to bear one another's burdens and naturally to care for each other. As they have daily a more intimate acquaintance with, so they have a more endeared affection for, each other."

Modern sociological studies confirm the pattern of Scripture and church history. Sociologists call fellowship groups "primary groups." Primary groups are characterized by intimate, face-to-face associations and cooperation. They are fundamental in forming the social nature and ideals of the individual. Primary groups mold the members' opinions, guide their affections, influence actions, and in a large measure determine their loyalties. They facilitate joint action for a common purpose.

The family, a circle of close friends, and a small Christian fellowship group are examples of the primary group. To sociologists, assimilation is the process by which an individual or group joins the life of another group and identifies with its goals. Assimilation, say the sociologists, takes place most rapidly where contacts are primary, that is, where the contacts are intimate and intense as in the family, small congenial groups, and close-touch relationships. To Christians in evangelism, this means that the best strategy is one that makes good use of small groups for fellowship and instruction. In order to become assimilated, new members need to gain a sense of belonging and identity as followers of Christ and members of His body, and small groups offer love, acceptance, and value-sharing in very effective ways.

Pastor's Class for Prospective Members

Assimilation of new members is not automatic, nor is it a one-time act. It is a continuing process that takes people's time, resources, and efforts. It is primarily the responsibility of the church, not of the new members. It is most successful when it *begins* before membership. Pastors need to take an active role in the assimilation program for new members.

A Prospective Member's Class is a very important ingredient in new member assimilation. Its purpose is to help the prospective member become an active and responsible member and one who has a personal sense of belonging and a desire to be useful in the life of the congregation.

In our congregation in Miami we offer a seven-week class led by the pastor. A high priority of this class is for each prospective member to build lasting relationships with other class members and to commit himself to a meaningful role or task ministry in the church. A role ministry is defined as a specific ongoing responsibility, such as ushering, visitation, and youth work. A task ministry is a short-term responsibility, such as participating in a church workday, bringing a meal to a shut-in, or some other one-time service.

During the course of the class, our goals for new member assimilation are spelled out clearly. If prospects commit themselves to membership, it is our responsibility to lead them into a small group fellowship within the first three months and to give them a role or task ministry within the first six months. During the sixth week of class, an assimilation survey is distributed and explained. The survey asks what type of small fellowship group they would like to join and reviews the number of role and task opportunities in the congregation. At that time the class members are encouraged to investigate the areas of ministry that interest them most.

Assimilation Committee

A key element in the assimilation of new members is the formation and function of an Assimilation Committee. A minimum of four members is needed for the committee. One member's responsibility is to channel new members into small fellowship groups. Another has the task of matching areas of interest in role and task ministry taken from the assimilation survey done during the sixth week. A third member keeps progress records on the new members, including their worship patterns, Sunday school attendance, small group involvement, role or task ministry, and financial giving.

The fourth member of the Assimilation Committee is the coordinator, who oversees the work of the committee and reports to the governing board of the church. The members of the committee should keep themselves thoroughly acquainted with the fellowship groups related to the church as well as the role and task opportunities available. The primary function of the Assimilation Committee is to meet and match individuals and couples with compatible fellowship groups in the church and to involve them in role and task ministries.

In order to do this efficiently, the Assimilation Committee must keep on hand an up-to-date listing of every group, activity, ministry, role, task, duty, and committee in the life of the congregation. They must know who the leaders and contact persons are for each ministry and activity. They must keep in touch with the various groups in order to know where the needs and openings are. They may often be surprised to discover that there are not as many opportunities for fellowship and ministry as they imagined. In such cases, they must create the openings! New groups should be organized and new projects developed in order to enlist the participation of every available person. If there are not enough small group fellowships to absorb the new members, a new fellowship should be created from the current members of the prospective member's class.

Above all, remember that personal relationships are the key to assimilation. Newcomers must interact with others in fellowship and ministry in order to gain their sense of belonging and the satisfaction of service. The assimilation process of new members must be monitored continually for at least a year, and any signs of regression quickly corrected. After the new member's first year anniversary in the congregation, the Assimilation Committee should review the record and ask itself, Is this person now an assimilated member of the church?

Barriers to New Member Assimilation

In many churches, membership is relatively easy to acquire. But few of the new members may actually be accepted into the life of the congregation. This means that a great number of people are left on the marginal edge of church relatedness. They came into the church expecting to be received and loved, but they never quite made it. Some kind of barrier separates them from penetrating the inner circle of congregational life. They sense it, though they probably can't identify the reason. It's painful, and it ought not be there.

Barrier identification is the first step toward solving the problem. Two types of barriers exist: church-related barriers and new-member-related barriers.

Church-Related Barriers

Time. As time passes, assimilation becomes more difficult. If too much time goes by from when a member enters the wider church fellowship to when he is invited to become a member of a small group, the chances are greatly diminished that he will take that step. When the new member approaches the church, he usually is open to new beginnings and new experiences. But if these don't appear within a short time, the new member becomes disillusioned, bored, and apathetic. He begins to fill his schedule with other things to do. At that point he is a high risk for dropout.

Structure. If there is no small group ready to receive him, and no role or task he can perform, the new member is up against a structural barrier that prevents his assimilation. The wise pastor and the efficient Assimilation Committee will make sure that there are fellowship groups ready for joining and service opportunities prepared in advance. Good planning and proper training and instruction for ministry facilitate the joy of feeling needed.

Win Arn, a leader in the American Church Growth movement, has pointed out that of the groups that now exist in any given church, one out of every five (20 percent) ought to have been started in the past two years. The reason is that groups tend to reach a "saturation point" somewhere between nine to eighteen months following their formation. In most cases, they will no longer be able to assimilate new people effectively. The only feasible remedy is the formation of new groups! The formula looks like this:

New groups = new growth = new people involved.

By continually developing new groups, new service projects, and new openings for ministry, there will never be a lack of opportunities for new members to become involved. On the other hand, if in a church the number of classes, groups, and programs remains the same, attendance and membership will level off.

Attitude. A wrong attitude is the most difficult barrier to overcome. We are dealing here with the attitude of the older member toward the new member, and the problem can be divided into two parts.

"Not our kind." The "not our kind" attitude may spring from social, ethnic, or cultural barriers that cause the newcomer to be viewed as undesirable and prevent his inclusion in the group. Some people refer to it as the "Homogeneous Unit Principle," which means in simple words that "birds of a feather flock together," and so do church members. It is a subtle form of exclusion and is essentially contrary to the gospel. Jesus opened the church door to birds of all kinds, and the members best honor their Lord by accepting and assimilating all who would come to the nest.

"Old versus new" members. When sociologists discuss the inclusion/exclusion factor within groups, they identify the hurdles newcomers

have to overcome. The "we" or in-group instinct positions itself against the "they" or out-group element. Within churches this describes the barrier between the new member and the older members. People who are already in the fellowship enjoy a feeling of unity and a sense of obligation toward each other. The very strength of their mutual feelings may constitute a barrier the newcomer must overcome.

New-Member-Related Barriers

The second barrier category is new member related. Here barriers may be emotional, spiritual, or relational.

The new member may erect an emotional barrier because he is just not ready to become involved in a new congregation. Usually this person is a more mature Christian who has transferred from a church with problems or who was so involved in his former church that he is now "burned out." This type of person was probably the Sunday school Superintendent, the Clerk of Session, or Committee Chairman of the Evangelism Visitation Committee, and pitcher on the church softball team just before he transferred his membership. He may need a time of emotional healing before he is ready for involvement in the church's new program.

A spiritual barrier may exist when the new member is not mature enough to understand the importance of fellowship and ministry. He just doesn't want to "get involved." His life up to this point has had a different priority structure, and a high degree of church involvement does not seem important to him.

There is also the possibililty of a relational barrier, which appears when the new member's spouse is not a believer or a church member. The spouse may forbid or hinder participation in small group fellowship, or the new member may simply not want to get involved without the mate.

Each of these situations requires special attention. Some barriers take a long time to remove. But in each case the pastor and other leaders of the congregation should try to identify the problem and seek to remedy it. Whatever prevents or hinders the free flow of the gospel to unchurched people and the joyful entry and assimilation of new members must be viewed as dishonoring to the Lord and a problem to be addressed.

There can be no greater joy and satisfaction for a congregation than to know that the new members are being fully accepted into the fellowship and are growing spiritually. For God intends His church to be a covenant community of "shared life," the abundant life of active participation with God and other believers.

Too often the missing link in congregational evangelism is a carefully planned and monitored program of assimilation. An assimilation program requires a great deal of time and effort on the part of older members, but the benefits are tremendous. In a confused, hostile, and dying world, there can be no beacon of light more powerful than a community of people who love and fellowship with one another. The fellowship of the church is God's foretaste of heaven on earth.

_10_

Equipping the Church for Lifestyle Evangelism
T. M. Moore

It is no secret that the broader evangelical church looks with suspicion upon the convictions of Reformed Christians to do evangelism. There are several reasons for such misgivings.

First, there is the general impression that Calvinists are content to fulfill their evangelistic obligations from behind a pulpit. Remarks such as those from the seventeenth-century Calvinist pastor John Owen may add force to this, for in his book, _The True Nature of a Gospel Church,_ Owen offers his opinion on the proper locus of evangelism:

> It is true, men may be, and often are, converted unto God by their occasional dispensation of the word who are not called to office . . . [but] the administration of the glorious gospel of the blessed God, as unto all ends of it, is committed unto the pastors of the church.

Owen apparently thought that the work of evangelism should be left mainly to those who are officially ordained to the pastoral office. As designated ministers of the gospel, they carry out the task of evangelism primarily, if not exclusively, through the official preaching of the Word, and this usually in church and on Sunday. This position has made considerable impact on Reformed circles, and every so often it surfaces in the form of resistance to any kind of lay evangelism. Reformed people who could not agree with this position have in the past gone off to other churches and mission organizations. Today Owen's view is at best a minority position within Reformed circles.

Perhaps the most misunderstanding and embarrassment regarding our interest in evangelism comes from an analysis of the growth patterns of Reformed denominations in North America and Europe over the last few decades. Evangelicalism as a whole has been enjoying a lively increase in membership. But the Reformed churches have not kept pace with their evangelical brethren. To be honest, our record does little to demonstrate a close tie between the Reformed faith and evangelism.

Whatever may be the causes of the dilemma, the obligation to correct our mistakes and to fulfill the God-given mandate of evangelism rests squarely on the shoulders of the Reformed churches. We must reexamine our practices and ask ourselves if we are pursuing the work of God's kingdom in a manner consistent with the teachings we hold dear.

Such passages as Ephesians 4:11-15 teach that authentic Christian churches will, without exception, be composed of members who are actively involved in declaring their faith to others, in "speaking the truth in love," as Paul expresses it. Their witness is not the exception, but the rule, and is the natural outgrowth of their maturing experience of God's grace and the work of the Spirit. The Lord Himself promised this when He said that the Holy Spirit within the believer would create a spontaneity of expression concerning spiritual and eternal matters (John 7:38-39).

My purpose in this chapter is to assist pastors and other church leaders to promote the organized, systematic witness of their members through lifestyle witnessing. In particular, four criteria for the development of effective lifestyle evangelism in the churches will be considered: the need for an effective model, the need for a means of encouraging lifestyle evangelism, the need for a commitment to the long haul, and the need for realistic expectations. I will look at each of these criteria separately.

Lifestyle Evangelism Defined

Let me define precisely what I mean by lifestyle evangelism. I do not mean the mere perpetuation of a program of "canned witnessing" as one of many programs in the local church. The "canned" approach involves recruiting lay men and women for weekly "outreach" sorties into homes of the neighborhood to present some static form of the gospel message, either by the reading or distributing of tracts, or the recitation of a memorized and often poorly understood outline of the gospel. Lifestyle evangelism may require some aspects of such a program at some point. But if such a program is all that eventuates, I can only say that the church has missed the point of lifestyle evangelism.

Moreover, I certainly do not mean some sort of annual outreach emphasis on the part of the local church, often in the form of an itinerant evangelist brought in to harangue the congregation and any neighbors who can be cajoled into attending. Although such endeavors may occasionally bear some fruit, they are not what I mean by lifestyle evangelism.

By lifestyle evangelism I mean *equipping the saints to bear effective testimony to the Lord Jesus Christ in the normal context of their everyday lives, through the formal and casual relationships in which they are involved, and in a manner and at a level that conforms to the needs and interests of their hearers.* Roland Allen had this in mind when he spoke of the "spontaneous expansion" of the Christian faith and how it starts: Spontaneous expansion begins with the individual effort of the Christian to assist his fellow, when common experience, common difficulties, common toil have first brought the two together. It is this equality and community of experience which makes the one deliver his message in terms which the other can understand, and makes the hearer approach the subject with sympathy and confidence."

In lifestyle evangelism, our concern is for a consistency of witnessing that finds its expression in daily living and takes into loving consideration the communicational needs of those we seek to evangelize, without compromising the truths of the gospel. What, then, is necessary to achieve this type of evangelism by church members?

Effective Models Needed

The first need is for effective models, alive and visible, in the local churches. Helmut Thielieke made the point well when he said,

"Today all the really vital questions that touch the depths of existence enter man's consciousness through the medium of persons in whom these questions are, as it were, incarnated."

Jesus was acutely aware of His role as a model of the type of behavior He desired for His followers. On at least two occasions He made this clear to them. On the eve of His crucifixion, Jesus encouraged the disciples to believe that all was not at an end, indeed, that the real work was just about to begin. With the coming of the Holy Spirit, He pointed out, all the mighty works His disciples had observed in Him would suddenly devolve upon them, and in an even greater degree (John 14:12-13). He encouraged them to believe that they could emulate His works with great effect, because of the power of the Holy Spirit at work in them. Again, after His resurrection, Jesus commissioned His disciples to go out into the world after the same pattern they had seen in Him (John 20:21). During the fifty days after Jesus' resurrection the disciples did a good deal of recollecting. The works they had seen Christ do were now to become characteristic of them. He had modeled the mission they must now undertake.

Paul revealed a conscious awareness of his modeling role. On numerous occasions he exhorted his disciples to be followers of him (cf. I Cor. 4:16; Phil. 3:17; I Thess. 1:6). Particularly in Philippians 3:17 does this self-consciousness seem evident: "Brethren, be followers together of me, and mark them which walk so as ye have us for an ensample" (KJV).

In churches today this responsibility to model the evangelistic way of life falls, primarily, upon those who follow in the footsteps of Jesus and Paul as the shepherds of the sheep. I apply this particularly to Reformed pastors who are seeking a way out of evangelistic doldrums. Unless pastors are willing to accept this responsibility and diligently make their evangelistic lifestyle one that their people can both observe and emulate, it is doubtful whether the membership will be able to make much progress in this most important calling. The servants cannot be expected to rise above the level of their masters, and the sheep will not follow a path on which they are not personally led.

The process of equipping the saints to speak the truth in love as a matter of everyday living must begin in the heart and life of the pastor. No "proven program" or clever combination of surrogate outreaches will long endure in the absence of an effective model of lifestyle evangelism.

Encouraging Christians to Lifestyle Evangelism

The second criterion involves developing and implementing a plan to equip church members for lifestyle evangelism. Ephesians 4:11-15 indicates that the saints are to be equipped ("perfected") for the witnessing way of life. This leads to a number of ancillary needs.

First, pastors must initiate and maintain such a plan. Paul maintains that pastor-teachers were given to the church in order to equip the saints. Thus, not only must pastors model the witnessing way of life, but they must also assume the responsibility for providing a plan and a context for equipping the people entrusted to their pastoral care.

It is impossible for pastors to escape the responsibility the Scriptures place on them. Nevertheless, the widespread lack of such equipping plans in the churches of the Reformed community bears stark testimony to our negligence in this area. We cannot simply respond that the overall training program of our churches is designed to produce such lifestyle witnessing. Such results are not in evidence. Our overall church programs are not doing what they are intended to do. A specific equipping plan cannot be left to our regular preaching and Sunday school instruction.

Second, an effective plan of equipping involves the need for incremental instruction in the nature and content of the gospel message itself. God's people need to learn what to testify. They need to learn it clearly, cogently, with repetition and evaluation, because many of them have great difficulty saying plainly what God in Christ does for sinners, especially to a non-Christian who does not know our jargon.

Again, this was a part of the equipping plan Jesus used with His disciples. Jesus spent the better part of three years teaching them God's truth and watching over the process of their coming to understand and communicate it. Since we are dealing here with one specific skill to be acquired, it may not be necessary for us to take

three years. But some sort of progressive learning process is necessary, and pastors need to lay out careful plans by which their people
can grow in understanding and ability over a designated period of
time.

Third, a plan of equipping must provide opportunities for the
learners to see the skill used in "real life" situations. This is why
Jesus felt it so necessary that His disciples be "with him" (Mark
3:14). Being "with him" provided the life-changing dynamic that,
later on, others observed in the disciples when they launched their
own evangelistic endeavor (Acts 4:13). Staged demonstrations of
evangelistic skills may have their place in an equipping plan, but
there is no substitute for the living demonstration of the ability to
testify to another person concerning the grace and power of the
Lord Jesus Christ.

Fourth, a plan of equipping must provide opportunities for the
learners to deploy their newly acquired skills gradually in a con-
trolled situation. Jesus sent His disciples out two by two and then
asked them to give Him an account of their labors. Our instruction in
lifestyle evangelism must involve a similar type of equipping, one in
which the learners may, in authentic witnessing situations, begin
gradually to express their witness to Jesus Christ. A proper context
will also include encouragement and feedback from those seeking to
transfer the skill to the learners.

Fifth, an effective plan of equipping must also include clear instruction on the work of the Holy Spirit in the evangelistic endeavor.
Learners must understand the Spirit's role as teacher, power supply, convictor, converter, and sealer of those who truly come to
faith. Only such instruction will enable us to avoid the pitfalls of
pressure tactics, guilt trips, and self-righteousness in evangelism.
By understanding the work of the Holy Spirit, we will be able to
keep our own roles in evangelism in proper perspective.

Sixth, an effective plan of equipping will promote an understanding of the people being evangelized so that the presentation of the
gospel message will be suited to their levels and needs. Paul's
example instructs us in this matter. In each case he took into account
the interests and world view of his audience, couching his evangelism in terms they would more readily understand. Paul took

effective communication seriously, and he obviously was sensitive to his hearers' interests and needs. Since evangelism is a matter of effective communication, the onus rests on those who would bear witness to take into account the needs of those they wish to reach. An effective plan of equipping will not omit this important consideration.

Seventh and finally, an effective plan of equipping takes seriously the role of the local church as both the means and the end of evangelism. That is, we must be prepared to introduce any converts into the life of the church as the body of Christ. We may not be content with leaving them to fend for themselves. They must be folded into the local church, where they can be nurtured spiritually and led to responsible discipleship.

Commitment to the Long Haul

The third criterion for bringing about lifestyle evangelism among church members is a commitment to the long haul. A congregation that is growing as a result of active witnessing to Jesus Christ will not appear overnight. Rather, it will require a long-term process of development. Paul was aware of this when he wrote to Timothy, "The things you have heard me say in the presence of many witnesses entrust to reliable men who will also be qualified to teach others" (II Tim. 2:2).

Two features in particular strike me in this verse. First, Paul attaches great importance to the transference of spiritual knowledge and skills from one generation of believers to the next, from the learned and equipped to the unlearned and unequipped. Timothy is exhorted to pass along the things he has previously learned from Paul.

Believers who have come to understand matters of faith and life, and have acquired particular skills in the work of ministry, must not be content with merely enjoying the fruits of their learning or deploying their skills in the service of the kingdom. *Rather, they are expected to seek a context in which they can transfer those skills and insights to a new generation of untrained believers, thus multiplying the benefits of their knowledge and gifts throughout the believing community and into succeeding generations.*

There is a sense of "ongoingness" about all kingdom work that precludes any notions of "instant equipping" or of taking a "one-shot" approach to the work God has given us to do. Equipping the saints to speak the truth in love is too big and important a work to be accomplished overnight. Regardless of failures and obstacles, the imperative to transfer our knowledge and skills to others is critical. Reformed pastors must find the vehicles by which to accomplish this transference.

Second, Paul demands the extension of his own knowledge and skills to no less than three generations beyond himself. The process can be diagramed as follows:

Paul
↓
Timothy
↓
Faithful Men
↓
Others Also

Paul was determined to transfer his knowledge and skills all the way to the third generation beyond himself. This required the involvement of those he had equipped, and others yet to be equipped, in the process. Certainly this required a long-range approach to the work of equipping the saints for witness and service.

Moreover, when we consider that Paul was involved in this process not only with Timothy, but with other followers as well, we see that the transference of his knowledge and skills was not merely linear but pyramidal, thus ensuring an increasingly broader base of equipped saints through the churches of the Roman Empire. Certainly we who aspire to follow in the tradition and pattern of the apostle Paul need to be committed to a long-term process of equipping the saints in all areas of Christian life and ministry, including that of lifestyle evangelism.

Realistic Expectations

Fourth and finally, in order to be able to provide for the equipping of the saints for lifestyle evangelism we need to have a realistic understanding of the kinds of results we can expect.

We are all familiar with the promises and guarantees given or implied in various witnessing strategies and programs. Their advocates write glowingly of their success records and project the image of having "sure-fire" ways of winning people to Christ and making the church grow. Such boasting is unwarranted. It is out of line with biblical teaching concerning the results we can expect.

Only the Holy Spirit can effect genuine conversions, and our only legitimate concern is the effective communication of the gospel. We pray that the Spirit will open doors and draw to Christ those to whom we bear witness. We do everything we can to communicate effectively so that no unnecessary barrier to understanding remains in the hearer's way. But beyond that, biblically speaking, we should not and cannot go. The final results of evangelism rest entirely in God's hands.

If, therefore, conversion is God's work and communication is ours, how can we know whether or not effective communication has in fact occurred? Scripture gives us helpful guidelines in answering this question. In Acts 17:22-34, the apostle Paul took special pains to make his gospel communication clear and cogent. Paul's hearers were sophisticated Athenians and worshipers of many gods. From the responses Paul received to his witness we get an idea of how to evaluate the effectiveness of our witnessing. Paul's witness on the Areopagus elicited three types of responses.

First, some rejected the claims of the gospel outright. They mocked the apostle, because they perceived his message as altogether outside the bounds that their world views would permit. *The point is not that they mocked, but that they understood the meaning and ramifications of Paul's message clearly enough to do so.* Evidently Paul had communicated clearly enough to this group that they knew what he was driving at. The fundamental difference between Paul's faith and their religious position had become clear in his presentation, and these hearers decided to reject what they heard.

Second, we find a group whose interest and curiosity had been sufficiently whetted to leave open the possibility of further discussion of the claims of the gospel. Something they heard in Paul's message, together with their own consciousness of need, engendered a halfway response that made possible a future inroad of the gospel.

Third, some members of the group received Paul's words with outright faith and commitment. The word of the gospel and the work of the Spirit found its mark in their lives, and they were converted.

It is from these three kinds of responses that we can measure our effectiveness in communicating the gospel. And every plan that intends to equip the saints effectively to speak the truth in love must be prepared for each of these contingencies. This means that as lifestyle evangelists we must be steeled against rejection and intimidation on the part of unbelievers. We must be prepared to develop new friendships and go the extra mile in the ongoing communication of the gospel. Our churches must be equipped to begin and carry through the process of Christian nurture in the lives of those brought to Christ as a result of our witnessing.

We cannot expect that fulfilling our responsibility to equip the saints for lifestyle evangelism will be a quick and easy task. Rather, pastors will have to commit themselves to careful study, personal effort and involvement, and exposure to failure. But the Lord stands ready to bless the energy we sincerely put forth in this most important area of kingdom work.

— 11 —

Hospitality Evangelism
Richard P. Kaufmann

In *Your Church Can Grow*, Peter Wagner sets forth the following hypothesis: "The effectiveness of the Christian's role as a witness for church growth decreases with that person's maturity in Christ." As a Christian matures in Christ he becomes more and more involved in the church. His free time is quickly filled with Christian activities such as worship services, prayer meetings, Bible studies, Sunday school, committee meetings, and church socials. Either his non-Christian friends are converted, or he gradually loses contact with them as their interests take them in different directions.

As a result, evangelistic programs based on members' inviting their friends often fail. They fail not because of poor planning, or poor scheduling, or poor programing, but because members have too few non-Christian contacts to invite.

New converts, however, are more effective as witnesses because they have more vital contacts with non-Christians. But often the new convert is not as effective as he could be because he does not think he is ready to share the gospel effectively. He may postpone witnessing until he has "learned more about the Bible." By the time he has acquired the amount of knowledge he thinks is necessary to present the gospel, he no longer has the same vital relations with non-Christians that he once had.

Hospitality evangelism addresses this problem. It aims at helping the more mature Christian develop meaningful contacts with non-Christians and helping the new convert continue to witness effectively to the contacts he already has. Hospitality evangelism helps your congregation grow as a warm, evangelizing church.

What Is Hospitality Evangelism?

The New Testament word for "hospitality" is a combination of two words that mean "love" and "stranger." Put this together with "evangelism," which is the proclamation of the good news about Jesus Christ. The goal of evangelism is to persuade men and women to trust in Jesus Christ as Lord and Savior and serve Him in the fellowship of His church.

Hospitality evangelism, then, is proclaiming the good news to those in your sphere of influence by hospitality and deeds of love and kindness, with the goal of their salvation and incorporation into a Christ-centered local church.

Note particularly that the *focus* of hospitality evangelism is your sphere of influence—your relatives, neighbors, classmates, fellow employees, and business associates. In other words, the people with whom you have regular and ongoing contact. Note also that the *means* of hospitality evangelism is love, friendship, and deeds of kindness.

The context of hospitality is extremely appropriate for sharing the gospel because we proclaim the good news that God has been hospitable to us through His Son, Jesus Christ. Christ's death and resurrection make it possible for people to enter into God's presence and experience His forgiveness, love, and hospitality. God truly loves strangers.

The people with whom you have contact in the neighborhood, at work, in school, and in clubs and organizations can be placed in one of three groups: (1) those whom you do not know (surprisingly most people do not know 50 percent or more of the people in their neighborhood); (2) those whom you know by name and can talk to about "the weather"; and (3) those with whom you have a fairly close, comfortable relationship.

Hospitality evangelism is a process by which we get to know people and develop trusting, loving relationships in order to be able to present the gospel to them. Thus the purpose of hospitality is for people to come to know Jesus Christ as their Lord and Savior. The greatest inherent problem in hospitality evangelism is seeing friendship as an end in itself. You must not be satisfied merely with making friends for yourself. Your purpose must be to help your friends become friends of Jesus.

Do you have friends to whom you have never presented your testimony and the gospel of Christ? Write down five names today and begin to pray for their salvation. Decide now to share what Jesus means to you with these individuals within the next two weeks. Hospitality evangelism begins with that important step.

Is Hospitality Evangelism Biblical?

There is a very clear biblical basis for practicing hospitality evangelism. Hospitality is one of the qualifications of a leader in Christ's church (I Tim. 3:2; Titus 1:8). The significance of hospitality is obvious when we see it listed with qualifications such as "above reproach, husband of one wife, temperate, prudent, respectable."

Not only leaders but all believers are commanded to be hospitable (Rom. 12:13; Heb. 13:2; I Pet. 4:9). Why is it so important to the Lord that you be hospitable? Because you represent a hospitable God. When God commands the Israelites to be hospitable (love strangers), the reason He gives is this: "for you were strangers in the land of Egypt: I am the Lord your God" (Lev. 19:34, RSV). That last clause is shorthand for "I am the Lord your God, who brought you out of the land of Egypt, out of the house of slavery" (Exod. 20:2, NASB). God had shown hospitality to them when they were strangers, and He calls them to do likewise. If you are a believer, you were a "stranger" (Eph. 2:12), but God has "delivered [you] from the domain of darkness, and transferred [you] to the kingdom of His beloved Son" (Col. 1:13, NASB).

When Jesus cried out, "It is finished!" (John 19:30), "the curtain of the temple was torn in two from top to bottom" (Mark 15:38). This began a great open house. God now welcomes us, and we can come continually "with confidence" into His presence (Heb. 4:16) and experience His love and hospitality. God calls us to be hospitable because He was first hospitable to us.

Hospitality is so important to God that His very purpose of redemption is often described in terms of it. Once all sin has been removed, the kingdom of Christ will be finally and fully ushered in and "in that day each of you will invite his neighbor to sit under his vine and fig tree, declares the Lord Almighty" (Zech. 3:10). That coming kingdom has dawned upon us with the resurrection of Christ. The coming age of hospitality has invaded this present evil age through the coming of the Holy Spirit. In a very real way when you have people into your home or welcome them at your church with the love of Jesus, it is a taste of heaven.

The kingdom of God is described as a banquet (Luke 13:29-30; 14:15-24; Rev. 19:9), and when the Lord returns, "He will dress himself to serve," and He will show hospitality to us, His guests (Luke 12:37).

In God's plan for bringing people into His eternal home the believer's hospitality plays a significant role. After the day of Pentecost, Christians were meeting in homes for teaching, fellowship, worship, and prayer. They "ate together with glad and sincere hearts, praising God" (Acts 2:46-47). These believers were sharing the Father's hospitality with one another, and things were happening: "The Lord added to their number daily those who were being saved" (Acts 2:47).

Evidently believers were inviting their friends who then heard the gospel in the context of love and hospitality. This is "John 13:35-hospitality-evangelism." Jesus says: "Love one another, even as I have loved you. . . . By this all men will know that you are my disciples, if you have love for one another" (John 13:34-35, NASB). The unbelievers saw the power of the gospel in the way the early Christians loved one another, and they wanted to be loved by that great love that flows from our Savior through us.

The apostle Paul, though often thought of primarily as a travelling missionary, also practiced hospitality evangelism. While he was held captive in Rome, he lived in a rented home, "and was welcoming all who came to him, preaching the kingdom of God, and teaching concerning the Lord Jesus Christ with all openness, unhindered" (Acts 28:30-31, NASB). Even if you are a shut-in, God will bring the mission field into your home if you commit yourself to share our hospitable Lord with others.

Hospitality is an important means of taking the gospel to the ends of the earth. Throughout the New Testament there is evidence that missionaries were welcomed into the homes of believers in order to reduce the cost of travel and to be strengthened in body and spirit.

Does Hospitality Evangelism Work?

Hospitality is an effective method of evangelism. In less than six years, over 300 people heard the gospel in our home. Over a two-year period more than fifty of our unchurched friends visited the church we attended as a result of the ministry of hospitality the Lord gave us. Twenty-two people now regularly attend that church because of our ministry of hospitality. And during that total six-year period of practicing hospitality, approximately forty people professed faith in Jesus Christ and are now active members of various churches. But this is only the beginning of a chain reaction set off and continued by the Holy Spirit. These converts have been used to bring the gospel to countless others through hospitality. Many have been saved and have continued sounding forth the good news.

Hospitality is an effective ministry of love. You may not see the evangelistic fruit that we have, or you may see much more. Either way, you will be involved in demonstrating the character of our loving God. What an exciting and faith-building experience it will be for you to watch Jesus love strangers through you! As you admit your own inability to be hospitable and depend on the Holy Spirit, you will be excited to see how loving you can be.

One night we prayed God would show us how to love a lonely elderly couple on our block. The next day I had all but forgotten them, but my daughters (Kristi was eight years old and Kim was seven at the time) had not forgotten. They picked some flowers, made a bouquet, and took it to this couple. This started a relationship through which Christ poured out His love abundantly, and it led to our sharing the gospel.

Hospitality evangelism is an effective way to unify and disciple your family. This kind of evangelism is a family project. A wise Lord has placed you and your family in a particular neighborhood and given you contacts at work and school for a purpose. He has given you and your family a mission field. Family devotions take on a new dimension when we pray for our neighbors. As a family we begin to see the lordship of Christ in all of life and the opportunities for witness that He sends our way. The way we love one another, mow our lawn, play with other children, and get involved in neighborhood events is a testimony to unbelievers. Discipling one another in this mission-oriented context brings real unity of spirit and purpose.

How to Do Hospitality Evangelism

Hospitality is not just another optional method of evangelism. As we have seen, all Christians are commanded to be hospitable in response to God's hospitality. But God does not require one specific way of practicing hospitality. God has made each of us different and put us in different neighborhoods and work and school situations. He commands us to be hospitable and then depend on Him for wisdom, guidance, and opportunities to express that hospitality.

I have found the following steps to be helpful in implementing hospitality evangelism in my life, family, and church.

1. Make a Household Commitment

This is a family project. If you do not live in a family, work on this project with your roommate, a Christian neighbor, or friends from church. In order to make a unified commitment, you will need first to transfer the vision to your family, or those with whom you work on the project. The most important aspect of the vision is the realization that a wise and sovereign God has placed you in your neighborhood, school, and place of employment *for a purpose.* We often complain about noisy neighbors and difficult school and work situations. ("How can I soar with eagles when I work with these turkeys?") But a loving, sovereign God makes no mistakes. He places you in strategic locations for the precise purpose of glorifying His name by your sharing of His love and the knowledge of the gospel of Christ. Look up I Peter 2:9–3:15 and reflect on its teaching. Your neighborhood and places of employment, school, and recreation are God-given mission fields that you can reach with the gospel more effectively than anyone else.

2. *Get to Know Your Neighbors*

Develop a strategy for getting to know people in your sphere of influence. For example, take a neighborhood prayer walk with your family, praying for each household. Make a map of your neighborhood, fill in the names you already know, and begin to pray for them.

We lived in one neighborhood for two and one-half years. The following chart will help you understand our strategy for getting to know our neighbors.

	Don't Know	Talking Basis	Close
9/1/76	80	0	0
10/1/77	60	10	10
11/1/77	20	50	10
2/1/78	20	35	25
2/1/79	10	40	30

When we moved in on September 1, 1976, we did not know any of our eighty neighbors (twenty-seven households). Thirteen months later, the progress had been disappointing. We had a commitment to reach our neighbors for Christ, but we had no plan. We decided to develop a strategy. Within one month we were able to meet and get to know forty additional neighbors. How did we do it? We held a neighborhood open house, for which we hand delivered the invitations. We found this to be a very effective way to begin to form relationships in a neighborhood where you do not know many people.

3. *Concentrate Your Efforts*

Prayerfully consider which people you think you can most effectively minister to at this time. "The number of people you can focus on may differ according to the amount of time you give to consciously sharing God's love. A busy executive, for example, may have time to work effectively with only one or two people at a time, whereas a retired person could easily focus on six or more non-Christians."[1] The quality of the relationship is more important than the quantity of people you work with.

Keep in mind also that this is not a once-for-all decision. Be open to God's leading through changing circumstances.

4. Develop a Ministry Plan

For each person on whom you are concentrating, develop a strategy to minister to his or her unique needs. Remember that Jesus lives in you and He wants to love this person through you with His unconditional, self-sacrificing love. With this fact and the uniqueness of the individual in mind, you are ready to develop a plan for expressing this love of Christ to the other person. Be wise and creative. Brainstorm with your family and Christian friends. Use the following suggestions to stimulate your thinking.

Let Your Light Shine. List any changes that you could make in order to be a better witness to this person. Try to look at yourself through the other person's eyes. What might be a stumbling block? What might enhance your testimony?

Do Deeds of Love and Kindness. Think of three specific deeds of love and kindness that you can do for this person that will communicate your love and concern for him or her in a meaningful way.

Build Friendship. Name three activities you can share with this person. They may be activities that will be new for both of you, things that you are presently doing, or projects you are working on and can enlist the other person's help for. Who else in your church has some of the same interests as this person? Who else in your church would seem to get along well with this person? Think of some activities in which you can include this person along with other people from the church. What church activities may be of interest to this person?

---

1. Arn and Arn, *The Master's Plan for Making Disciples* (Pasadena, Calif.: Church Growth Press).

Share Your Faith. What aspects of your own spiritual journey will this person be especially interested in? What felt needs does this person have that Jesus can meet?

As God draws men and women to Himself through these steps, involve them with you in the ministry of hospitality evangelism. New converts will have many vital contacts with unbelievers, so begin right away to assist them in reaching their unsaved friends with the good news.

5. Form an Accountability Group

I am convinced that one of the most significant steps you can take in implementing hospitality evangelism is to join with other believers to encourage, share, and support one another with prayer and other kinds of help.

At our church we have formed small groups for this purpose. Participants begin by attending a seminar on hospitality evangelism in which they learn what it is, why they should do it, and how they can do it. The seminar includes time for them to develop a ministry plan for each of the people on whom they are concentrating. After the seminar, participants meet weekly in small groups. The meetings are a time for sharing progress reports, prayer requests, and plans for hospitality ministry.

This evangelistic thrust has added an exciting dimension to the small groups that already existed in our church, and the small groups have helped us follow through on our hospitality evangelism strategy.

Putting Hospitality Evangelism Into Perspective

More important than the actual procedure of hospitality evangelism is the perspective on which hospitality evangelism is based. You may not see the fruit of your labors. You may experience various forms of opposition. At times you may be fearful. When this occurs, having the proper perspective is the key to perseverance.

Late one night I brought home a hitchhiker who needed a place to stay for the night. Our children were in bed asleep. My wife and I decided it would be best for our guest to sleep in our bedroom, and we slept in an extra room. I had been sound asleep when I was awakened by a terrifying scream. Immediately, I knew what had happened. Our daughter, who was then eight years old, woke up during the night and walked into her parents' bedroom over to a sleeping person who she thought was her father and touched him to awaken him. Our guest sat up with a start, and our daughter quickly realized that this man was not her father. He had a mustache—I don't; he had black skin—I don't. She let out a scream that was surpassed only by the scream of our guest.

As I comforted our daughter in my arms, I thought I had probably made an awful mistake by inviting this man to spend the night and that the trauma of that experience would cause lasting fears in my daughter.

The next day I spent some time alone with her to try to help her deal with what had happened. I did not know what to say, and so I read the words of Jesus to her, "Come, you who are blessed of my Father, inherit the kingdom prepared for you from the foundation of the world. For . . . *I* was a *stranger,* and you invited Me in; . . . truly I say to you, to the extent that you did it to one of these brothers of Mine, even the least of them, you did it to Me" (Matt. 25:34-35, 40, NASB).

I then asked, "Do you think we did the right thing?" She smiled and answered, "Yes." As far as I know she has never experienced nightmares or fears as a result of what occurred that night. The grace and truth of our Lord healed her.

This then is the perspective of hospitality evangelism: you are doing your hospitality and deeds of love and kindness to and for Jesus. You are doing it in response to the fact that Jesus loves you and gave His life for you so that you can experience God's love, forgiveness, and yes—His hospitality.

___ *12* ___

An Integrated Plan
for Evangelism and Church Growth
Terry L. Gyger

Over the past twenty years we have seen an avalanche of books, films, and seminars on church growth. Pastors hop from one seminar to another, trying to find the ideal approach that will make their congregations grow. We study models of "successful" churches intently and scrutinize their methods in the hope of uncovering formulas that can be applied elsewhere. All of this is evidence that churches today desire to grow, they are demanding growth leadership from their pastors, and pastors feel the pressure to find formulas for success.

However, churches do not grow because someone has discovered a particular method or formula for success. Not even a favorable neighborhood environment is any guarantee of success. Churches grow because of a combination of factors, each of which contributes in its own way. When successful churches are studied in depth, they reveal numerous factors that contribute to their health and vitality. They have ministries that at first glance do not seem important but, on closer examination, play important roles.

This is called the *multi-dimensional cause of church growth*, and when we look at its implications seriously, we uncover a major operating principle for pastoral leadership and church planning. Because this view focuses on the wide variety of causes of church health and growth, it avoids many of the common mistakes pastors and churches make. It seeks to integrate the whole life and witness of the church in a balanced and coordinated way.

Before going further, I want to point out a distinction between evangelism and numerical church growth. All Christians, at least theoretically, agree that evangelism is essential for the church. It is a mandate of the Lord and is not optional. Evangelism must be carried out faithfully because the head of the church has commanded it, whether the efforts put forth result in numerical church growth or not. From this viewpoint, some churches deserve more respect than they often receive because they are being evangelistically faithful despite their lack of numerical growth.

For example, church A may carry on powerful evangelism in a number of ways and yet not experience numerical growth in the membership because of factors beyond its control. In contrast, church B may be growing numerically without doing evangelism at all. It stands in a favorable location, where even mediocre performance yields growth. Church B basks in the glow of growth through transfer while not doing evangelism at all; church A fights a terrific battle against all kinds of obstacles, wins many to Christ, but on the growth charts looks poor. These differences need to be pointed out early in our discussion, and both credit and admonishment placed where deserved. Just because a particular church grows externally does not mean that it is meeting the demands of an integrated, multi-dimensional evangelism plan or that it is fulfilling its calling as a church of Christ. The faithful church will seek to identify all the factors contributing to health and growth and add the missing dimensions.

Obstacles Along the Road to Growth

The first obstacle is a common one and probably has done more harm to congregational evangelism than anyone realizes. It stems from a *narrow view of the nature of evangelism and the subsequent failure to mobilize all the members of the congregation.*

For example, a pastor may begin a plan of evangelism by seeking to recruit workers for door to door visitation. Maybe 5 percent of the membership responds, leaving the other 95 percent feeling guilty, inadequate, and probably a little hostile. Soon the Church has an elite core of confrontational, door-to-door evangelists, but also a large number of members convinced that evangelism is not for them.

This division is unfortunate to say the least. Confrontational evangelism is not the only kind of evangelism, nor is visitation the only method, nor are all Christians gifted in the same way. What every church needs is a multi-dimensional approach that utilizes all the members with their varied gifts and strengths. Confrontational evangelists are important, and more are needed. But so are the many other lay people who can contribute to the growth of the church by penetrating the community in other ways, building relationships and inviting friends and acquaintances to church. This wider group is, in fact, evangelism's crucial resource.

Elitism in any form is a dangerous thing, and it can happen very easily when we consider evangelism too narrowly. Evangelism that matches the gifts of only a fraction of the membership should not be elevated as the highest or exclusive method of witnessing, nor does it alone contribute to church growth. Pride on the one hand and jealousy on the other can erupt in a congregation that sets evangelism apart in an elitist fashion from the whole life and witness of the body. Division and decline eventually follow, and effort that was intended to produce church growth leads to church death. But in healthy, growing congregations all the differing parts of the church's life and ministry are encouraged and integrated in such a way that they contribute to the welfare of the whole.

The second obstacle is *notable but limited success*. This is a tricky one. Success in one or more areas may lead us to overlook an inherent weakness in another. For example, a pastor may be very successful in preaching and conducting public worship services, but weak in follow-up. People in the community are attracted by his preaching, and the worship services regularly have many visitors. But actual membership does not grow because the pastor's success in the worship services is not matched by an effective follow-up ministry. He fails to provide the kind of organizational leadership that enhances church growth.

For another example, some church members are especially gifted in initiating and building good relational bridges with outsiders, and friendship between Christians and non-Christians is often the first step for evangelism. But how does a person get from the outer perimeter to active membership? The answer is not as easy as we may think. Many converts find it difficult, sometimes impossible, to break through the invisible barriers to fellowship we have in our churches because the kind of discipleship that produces active, responsible church members is missing.

Wise pastors will work to keep the pipeline open between active church members and the people on the outside who are being drawn toward the church through the contacts and witness of the members. For new Christians to find a home in the church, there has to be an integrated program of evangelism, discipleship, and fellowship.

The third obstacle, *duplicated effort,* appears when there is no coordination between the various parts of the church program. The church's ministry includes many things that can contribute effectively to evangelism and growth if these elements are intentionally included and promoted.

For example, many churches are using growth cells for spiritual growth and fellowship. Growth cells can also be used for evangelism when the pastor emphasizes the importance of outreach and the members modify the character of the growth cell to include evangelistic ministry. The training for leading a small group applies just as much to an inductive evangelistic Bible study for inquirers as to a discipleship study for Christians. The same small group can edify the believer and be the door to Christ and the church for the newcomer.

Another example is the Sunday worship service. When worship includes the clear presentation of the gospel message as well as "meat" for mature members, the service becomes both an evangelistic event and an experience of praise and thanksgiving. Some of the most effective evangelism actually takes place in precisely that context. On the other hand, when the evangelism program is left to itself, uncoordinated with the rest of the things the church does, many efforts have to be duplicated, and energy and opportunities are lost.

The fourth obstacle applies especially to churches that are doctrinally orthodox, but evangelistically dead. They are "depth" churches full of individuals who "know theology," but lack the glow of spiritual warmth and closeness to Christ that would draw the lost and hurting to them. The only kind of growth such churches know is *biological* growth, through their children. To that end they emphasize instruction and separation. Their only hope is that their children will remain loyal to the church, and for that purpose they doctrinally galvanize them against defection. Few leave such churches through the back door, but no one comes in through the front door either. Whatever else they are, these churches are seriously lacking in basic biblical dimensions. They have stumbled over the obstacle of a *false dichotomy* between evangelism and discipleship, quality and quantity, doctrine and life.

The greatest challenge of the church today is to increase the percentage of its growth through conversions. Not by *transfer* growth, which means the attracting of members from other churches, but by *evangelistic* growth, the effective Spirit-blessed communication of the gospel to non-Christians that leads to active and responsible church membership. That is the kind of growth we need to emphasize. It is the area in which most churches are weakest.

Growth of many kinds is vital to Christian faith and life. Believers are commanded in Scripture to grow in grace and in the knowledge of the Lord Jesus Christ (II Pet. 3:18). The believer's spiritual growth relates to every other kind of growth, and it involves the three dimensions of knowing, doing, and being. Spiritually mature believers will not only study the Scriptures; they will obey the Scriptures. They will learn and discern true doctrine, and they will reach out to their neighbors. Love for their neighbors will lead them to do for their neighbors what is best for them, physically, emotionally, and spiritually.

The fifth obstacle has to do with spiritual gifts and the development of leadership. *The neglect of the members' varied gifts,* and the failure to develop leadership based on these gifts, is a trap into which many pastors fall.

Without functional growth, the church will never realize its full potential. Functional growth includes two aspects: the development of leaders (Acts 14:22-23) and the utilization of the spiritual gifts of all the members (I Cor. 12; Rom. 12). When pastors concentrate on equipping members through preaching, teaching, and discipling, and on motivating members to function to the fullest in their gift areas, the church grows naturally, and the members feel they are contributing significantly toward their common calling.

Key Elements of an Integrated Model

If you set out to build an integrated model of evangelism and church growth, there are certain key ideas you must work out.

1. *Ministry Must Be Multi-Dimensional.* You must strive to build a model that incorporates a variety of ministries. Ample provision must be made for prayer, fellowship, bridge building to non-Christians, worship, discipleship, and evangelism in various forms. Ministries of mercy are important and should be appropriate to the needs in the area.

In the Reformed community we maintain that public worship is to be Godward. Praise and thanksgiving are to be performed by true believers who hear God's Word for their lives and respond in praise and obedience. But can this worship be attractive to inquirers, the unchurched, and the uncommitted? In many large, growing churches the worship service is the public contact point for new people and becomes the entry point through which they are exposed to the gospel and the church's fellowship. Is something lost, from the Reformed perspective, when the public worship of God is designed to serve the purpose of evangelism as well as the praise of God and the edification of believers?

Our answer is that a truly worshiping church is a powerful witness to the unsaved and uncommitted. Invitations to attend worship are, in many instances, the first and most important efforts in evangelism for Christians. If, on the one hand, worship services are dull and unintelligible, without application to life, members will not feel inclined to invite friends and neighbors. But, on the other hand, if the gospel is proclaimed powerfully and winsomely, accompanied by joyful singing, prayers, and the spirit of true worship, believers will be strengthened in their faith and in their desire to invite outsiders to the services.

The same can be said of almost all the internal activities of the church. They are carried on for the benefit of Christians, and they also have dimensions of witness and evangelism.

2. Ministries Must Be Tailored to Fit Local Cultures. The creation of indigenous programs is another essential element if we want the church to grow in different cultures and socioeconomic groups. In basic philosophy and implementation of ministry, there are more similarities than dissimilarities among the growing congregations in North America. At the same time allowances, even of major significance, should be encouraged. If we want to see the church grow among all the different cultural groups of this and other countries, our ministries and the way we conduct them must be tailored to fit the specific cultures.

Presbyterians, for example, have not been very effective in planting the church in the subcultures of this continent. A large part of the problem stems from the reluctance of Presbyterians to make the adaptations necessary to fit cultures other than those in which Presbyterians traditionally are found. Our forms are too rigid, and we have clung to them beyond spiritual warrant. It is important for those working among people of other cultures to take the principles presented in this book and work them out creatively with indigenous leaders within the other cultures.

3. The Goal Must Be Total Mobilization. When I say that the total mobilization of the church for evangelism and growth should be the goal, I do not mean that every member is supposed to go out on Tuesday night in evangelistic visitation. We must respect individual gifts, callings, and personal preferences. Yet all who serve Christ faithfully, with commitment to excellence, are participants in growth and outreach.

For example, the nursery worker who commits himself or herself to excellence in child care is a growth participant. The married couple that functions as a friendship team to entertain and involve visitors in the church is an important growth factor. The single who invites fellow apartment dwellers to a religious retreat in the mountains is a growth participant. The young college student who coaches a junior soccer team is a growth worker. In short, every member can and should contribute to the internal and external growth of the church. Every member should be thinking growth, thinking ministry, thinking evangelism. Growth is the responsibility not of a few, but of all. Growth is never the result of one method, but the result of many. Growth participants are all the members who become mobilized for ministry, both inward and outward, each one according to his or her own personality, gifts, and maturity in Christ.

Michael Green, in his book *Evangelism in the Early Church,* shows that in the early years of the church, God used a host of methods to draw people to Himself and make the church grow. Is the church today as open to a variety of methods? Do we understand and appreciate the uniqueness of the various peoples we try to reach, disciple, and train? Do we value the many different gifts the Spirit bestows in the body, and are we willing to build creative strategies in which even timid believers can play a part and exercise their gifts?

4. Grassroots Leadership Must Be Developed. The development of local Christian leaders is a key element in any growth strategy. Outside experts, no matter how attractive and creative they may be, can never be the primary leaders or continual resource people in the church. Grassroots leaders must be produced and multiplied for healthy, sustained growth to occur.

It is easy to explain how a church can grow in size under the leadership of a strong individual. But it is impossible for a church to grow in spiritual depth and in multiple dimensions of ministry without the multiplication of leaders. This means for most churches the development of a decentralized strategy built on small groups. Small groups need leaders, and through the development of these leaders the entire church is strengthened.

5. Training Must Go From the Simplest to the More Complex. In good pedagogy the training elements move from the simplest to the more complex, and the same approach must be followed in mobilizing a church for evangelism and growth. Sensitive pastors realize that people in the pews can easily be intimidated. If pushed too far, too fast, they fall into a negative pattern of rejecting every new idea that is proposed.

Pastors must take people where they are and move them gently, beginning with simple tasks, toward the integrated congregational evangelism they have set as the goal. For example, pastors make a big mistake if they try to recruit, train, and deploy a large number of people directly into visitation evangelism. Most members simply are not ready for it, and a lot of our difficulties come as a result of our failure to understand where our people are in thinking and development. In most instances we have to go back to basics and teach people how to pray, trust, and take "baby steps" in outreach before we can expect them to make giant strides toward church growth. We must train them to be hospitable to one another before we can teach them to exercise hospitality to non-Christians. We must lead them to show friendship to visitors before we can expect them to build solid friendships with outsiders. In each area of church life, the process must go from the simplest things to the more complex.

6. *The Model of Growth for the Local Church Should Be Expandable.* Depending on its size and the strength of its leadership, a congregation should be able to begin with one or two program components and build from there. The initial endeavors should be done well, and each participant should be made to feel that his or her efforts are contributing significantly toward the growth of the church. The important thing to keep in mind is that beginning small does not mean remaining small. Additional parts of the integrated strategy can be added in later stages. Pastors should resist the temptation to add new programs before the early efforts have taken hold in the congregation and have been adequately developed.

7. *A Cyclical Pattern Works Best in the Average Congregation.* People like to know what they can expect, and therefore a cyclical pattern works best in the total strategy. Growing churches are not built on programs that are tried and then abandoned. Consistent programing, however, guarantees a cumulative effect.

A recycling program has four distinct advantages: (1) It sustains interest. People come to anticipate the repetitive program, especially when they enjoyed it and saw that it was successful. (2) It facilitates learning. A standardized approach conducted in a repetitive manner promotes comprehension and efficiency. (3) It builds impact. A continuing program builds up strength, and even in difficult situations it is supported by the knowledge and confidence of the members and grows in its effect on the congregation. (4) It develops recruits. It allows new believers to become involved and trains new leaders.

8. A variety of recruitment methods should be employed. In this congregational strategy for evangelism and growth, the goal is total mobilization. This means that recruitment, the enlistment of members for service and outreach, is an ongoing requirement. To this end a variety of recruiting methods need to be used.

Some enlistment techniques will have high visibility, especially those which seek to involve every believer in certain efforts. Other methods call for behind the scenes, person-to-person enlistment. For example, participants in a visitation program of evangelism should not be recruited from the pulpit. A public effort to recruit workers for that type of ministry usually has limited success and may deepen the evangelistic fright of some of the hearers.

A Look at the Charts

How does a pastor describe in a single chart or diagram all the activities and programs carried on by his church? The complexity of the average church is amazing. A lot goes on that can never be charted or described.

In the diagram included in this chapter I have attempted to describe in a graphic way the integrated approach to congregational evangelism and growth. Readers should remember that not all the activities occur at the same time, not even in the same calendar year. The program expands as the members learn, feel confident, and become increasingly involved. Some activities are focused primarily at discipling believers, while others aim more directly at evangelism. Discipleship and evangelism are never entirely separated, and the total life of the church is "arrowed" toward its ongoing witness to the world in the service of the Lord.

The most helpful thing for the reader/pastor to do is to take this diagram and use it as a model for producing a similar chart of his own church's plan for ministry. Remember that churches prosper and grow because of a combination of factors, each of which contributes in a significant way. The pastor's task is to provide the leadership that will integrate every facet of the church's work toward spiritual health and evangelistic growth.

AN INTEGRATED PLAN

ACTIVITY DESCRIPTION	VALUE	GROWTH ASPECT	INTEGRATION FACTOR(s)	INVOLVEMENT GOAL	TIME OF WEEK, PERIOD OF YEAR
A weekly cele-bration "event" attractive for outsiders and deeply meaningful for believers, done in excellence.	Primary, *worship* Secondary, *outreach*	Members are enthused about worship and invite neighbors, contacts, and friends. This event becomes an entry point to evangelism and church integration.	Celebration events are the "entry points" for new people and link them to fellow-ship activities.	100% (This event can grow as large as possible without weakening the church).	Continuous throughout the year. Prime time — 11:00 A.M. Sunday.
A 5-dimensional approach to build fellowship and true body life. Groups have 40–60 individuals.	*Fellowship*	Individuals build relationships/ friendships; personal needs are met; gifts are discovered; people feel significant.	People whose needs are met will invite others and talk favorably about the church. New people are integrated into church life. This provides growth in depth and breadth.	80%	Every week at second prime time — 9:30 A.M. Sunday.
Small groups of 8-14 individuals, meeting weekly for discipleship, study, prayer, accounta-bility, fellowship. *Bonding cell—* integrating new people. *Discipleship cell —* learning, applying. *Outreach cells —* evangelism through Bible studies.	Primary, *discipleship* Secondary, *evangelism, fellowship*	New people are integrated, trained involved. Out-reach cells are used for contact-ing and winning new people.	If individuals have a good experience in the community groups, it will be easier for them to attend a cell, and if they attend, they will see the integration be-tween evangelism, discipleship, and fellowship.	60%	Sunday night or during the week, (breakfasts, lunch-eons, evenings, etc.). Meet for designated period and then break. Periods range 4–12 weeks.
Teams of 2 people (couple or 2 men or 2 women) commit themselves to inte-grating new people through a 5-step process of reaching unchurched people through 5 steps of friendship building.	Primary, *evangelism* Secondary, *fellowship and visitor integration*	Many individuals visit the church, and personal attention and friendship will guarantee they stay. New relation-ships are built to non-Christians thus developing a growing network of contacts.	New relationships become opportunities for evangelistic presentations. New people who are well satisfied will invite others, thus develping a further network system. Individuals who go through this stage will be trainable in other tools for evangelism.	30%	Trained on Sunday night, they actually do their work on their own schedules.
Individuals are trained in an inten-sive way to do person-to-person evangelism and discipleship.	Primary, *evangelism* Secondary, *discipleship*	People are taken step by step through friendship outreach, then to intensive training in personal witnessing. People who are won to Christ can then be individually discipled.	Individuals come to worship . . . there is a need for friendship (*teams*), a need for discipleship (*cells*), a need for evangelism (*individuals trained to do this special work*).	10%	Trained through the week for at least 12-16 weeks. Evan-gelism training done with groups and with trainers. Dis-cipleship training done one on one, or one on two.

FOR EVANGELISM AND CHURCH GROWTH

VEHICLES OF
IMPLEMENTATION

TIME LINE

CONGREGATION

PARTICIPATION 100%

CELEBRATION
WORSHIP

1. "Focal point" of worship for Christians.
2. "Attractive point" — Christians bring friends, neighbors, etc.
3. "Entry point" to other ministries.

COMMUNITIES

PARTICIPATION 80%

FELLOWSHIP

BODY LIFE

TEACHING

Encouraging every member to be part of a mid-size community; 40–60 individuals.

CELLS

PARTICIPATION 60%

| 4 weeks BONDING CELL FELLOWSHIP | 12 weeks DISCIPLESHIP CELL Beginners and Advanced | 12 weeks EVANGELISTIC CELL |

TEAMS

PARTICIPATION 30%

FRIENDSHIP WITH VISITORS — 5 week commitment 5 steps of implementation

FRIENDSHIPS WITH COMMUNITY CONTACTS — Creative approaches done on one's own schedule

OUTREACH EVENTS

"FOCUS EVENTS"—Primarily to build relationships and present the gospel in need-oriented settings; 2–4 times per year.

BREAKFASTS
LUNCHEONS
MARRIAGE RETREATS

SEASONAL CONCERTS
DRAMA
COUPLES' BANQUETS

INDIVIDUALS

PARTICIPATION 10%

EVANGELISTIC APPOINTMENTS

DISCIPLESHIP—INTENSIVE 12–24 wks.

NOTES ON THE MODEL:
1. Solid lines represent recruitment at public meetings; broken lines represent recruitment done on a person-to-person basis.
2. Activities move from the least difficult to the most difficult in terms of involvement.
3. Activities move from the highest participation to the lowest participation.

___ 13 ___

Revitalizing a Dying Church
Harry L. Reeder III

"Revitalize a dying church!" In other words, be an instrument in the hands of God to breathe spiritual life back into a body before it becomes a corpse. For me this subject is both exciting and relevant. Why? For two reasons. First, because this has been my ministry, calling, and challenge, first at Pinelands Presbyterian Church in Miami, Florida, and more recently at Christ Covenant in Charlotte, North Carolina. Further, I suspect that most pastors in the course of their ministries will face the challenge of revitalizing a dying church. Even more specifically, the majority of seminary students who enter pastoral ministry upon graduation will confront the task of church revitalization.

Let me explain why. In working through a basic philosophy of ministry for myself as a pastor I have come to some conclusions. The key passage of Scripture for identifying a general approach to the pastoral ministry is Ephesians 4:11-16. The role commended to us is that of "pastor-teacher." The purpose is "to equip the saints for the work of the ministry" (v. 12, RSV). The method is twofold. First is an expositional public ministry of the Word that is faithful to the Scriptures, clear, and applicatory. Second is the occupation of discipling leaders who will multiply our ministry as they disciple others, who in turn disciple still others (II Tim. 2:23). I will say more about this later.

With those givens, I began to think about what types of pastorates there are. There are all kinds of pastoral ministries, and they all are challenging. But for the sake of analysis I have classified pastoral ministries into three basic categories.

1. *The Organizing Pastor.* The role of organizing pastor is a special calling for pastor-teachers who can both evangelize and equip. Clearly they must be effective leaders, capable, secure, creative, and self-starting. I think this category can be divided between organizing pastors who begin a work and then move on when it gets to a point of viability, and organizing pastors who begin a work and then stay with it even for a lifetime ministry. To be aware of one's strengths and limitations is vital in making this decision.

2. *The Continuing Pastor.* Continuing pastors are likewise of a special breed. They are pastor-teachers who are capable, effective, and secure about themselves. They succeed organizing pastors and minister in growing or basically healthy churches.

3. *The Revitalization Pastor.* Until recently I called this category the *Reclamation Pastor*, but the idea is the same. A once-flourishing church is on the decline to some degree. The people call a pastor who they hope will bring them back to the glory days. The pitfalls, challenges, and opportunities in this type of ministry are what I want to write about in this chapter.

Let me make a couple of observations. First, to be honest, only a few people have the discipline, character, skills, and spiritual gifts to be organizing pastors. And, therefore, my advice to any one pastor or seminarian is that he not accept a call to become an organizing pastor just because he does not get any other invitation and this seems to be his only option. Second, there are fewer healthy, growing, and successful pastorates available than you may think, and even fewer will be offered to graduating seminarians going into their first pastorates. Since there is no such thing as a "plateaued" church, the rest of the field is filled with churches that are experiencing spiritual decline or decay to some degree and, therefore, need a revitalization ministry. From personal experience I can say that to place yourself in the hand of God as His servant seeking to reverse the downward spiral of spiritual ineffectiveness of a congregation and to help it recapture the pattern of growth, momentum, enthusiasm, and optimism is an exciting challenge. And it is also a highly satisfying ministry. For by God's grace, tired old church can be revitalized!

Scriptural Data: The Seven Churches of Revelation

For scriptural data on the subject, we need go no further than five of the seven churches in Revelation 2 and 3, specifically Ephesus, Pergamum, Thyatira, Sardis, and Laodicea. Let us use the church at Ephesus as a case study of revitalization, using Acts 18, the Epistle to the Ephesians, I and II Timothy, and Revelation 2:1-7.

Ephesus was a church with noble beginnings through Aquila and Priscilla, the developing work of Apollos, and the three-year ministry of the apostle Paul. The synagogue was evangelized as they took the gospel first to the Jews. Then they went to the Gentiles, in the market place, and soon "the Word of the Lord was growing mightily and prevailing." Idol-makers were put out of business and the practitioners of the occult saw their books burned and their tricks and superstitions unmasked in public. As a result, Ephesus became a mother church sending evangelists throughout the region and planting numerous daughter churches. Paul concluded his planting ministry with his speech to the elders, recorded in Acts 20:17-35. In the midst of great affection and emotion he challenged them as shepherds of the flock and warned them of dangers to come. Finally, his ministry included a powerful letter, a kind of discipleship tool, setting forth the deepest doctrinal truths and the glories of Christ and His church. We all know this letter as the Epistle to the Ephesians.

The next thing we hear about Ephesus is in I and II Timothy. The apostle Paul had left at Ephesus his most trusted and effective disciple, Timothy, for a continuing and already a revitalizing ministry. Trouble had broken out as false teachers were turning the hearts of church members to false doctrine and practices.

A final exhortation toward revitalization, the strongest of all, comes from Jesus Himself, through the pen of the apostle John in the book of Revelation. A whole generation has passed, and the great church at Ephesus has fallen from the heights (Rev. 2:5). Its past record was so outstanding in obedient service, stalwart defense of sound doctrine, enduring hardship, and perseverance. But now to that church, with such a history, comes the terrible indictment that it has forsaken its first love and is in imminent danger of God's severest punishment.

What conclusions do we draw from this? *Revitalization is necessary in every church as each successive generation must personally commit itself to God, the Word, and the biblical mandate to make disciples of all the nations.* If a church of the caliber of Ephesus, with a history of such great leaders and ministries, could drift so far away in just one generation, it can happen anywhere, to any church, and invariably does.

Depressing Scenario of a Dying Church

Before I begin to apply some of the lessons learned from Scripture and personal, pastoral experience in this work of church revitalization, I want to lead you to *feel* what a dying church is like and the natural fear that grips you when you consider becoming its pastor and turning it around. The following true scenario is meant to help you place yourself in the very situation described and, I hope, on the threshold of a revitalization ministry.

A church in Florida calls you to be its pastor. This particular church was at one time among the largest and fastest growing in the region. It had risen to a membership of almost 900, with four major worship services and a vital Sunday school program marking the activities of each Lord's Day. It was known for creativity, an innovative youth program, an expanding Christian day school, and a clear commitment to world missions.

Now, twenty-five years later, the average Sunday morning attendance is below fifty. The Sunday school has fallen to less than twenty adults and four or five children. None of the children have parents attending the church. Sunday evening services have been cancelled and if four people come to mid-week prayer service, that is considered a notable victory. Vandalism occurs daily on the church grounds, and the budget has not been met for three years. Minimal amounts of money are now going to missions and benevolence. The

Christian day school has supported the church with its meager surplus, yet not one student's family or faculty member is attending the church.

The neighborhood around the church is in transition from white collar to blue collar. It is rapidly being repopulated by a diverse number of nationalities, representing a wide range of cultures, mostly from Caribbean countries and South America. The church building is located on a secondary road that abruptly comes to a dead end. Other factors could be mentioned that contributed to the church's decline, but they would involve personalities and disciplinary situations that should remain confidential. But I add one final item to this already depressing scenario. The average age of the congregation is in the upper fifties. You, the pastor, at the age of thirty-three, are the youngest person in the congregation apart from your wife and children.

Adding to your feeling of depression is the advice of the experts. Church growth consultants have already analyzed the church and have recommended one of two options. One is "close the doors, sell the property, and cut your losses." The second is "sell the property and move to a new location in a better neighborhood that has some element of homogeneity upon which you can build a church."

This is not a hypothetical example! This is Pinelands Presbyterian Church in 1980, the year the Lord called me to serve these dear people as their pastor. I knew in my heart that the experts were wrong, that the doors of Pinelands did not need to be closed, nor the neighborhood abandoned by the church. I was even more certain when a more appealing call to another church began to develop at the last moment. I knew it was diversionary, a test of fidelity. Did I really believe our Lord could and would do a "new thing" at Pinelands Church? For God's grace and power, and the flexibility and patience of the fifty "remnant" members, I am eternally grateful. Together we proved that old, sick churches don't have to die or flee to more friendly locations. They can be revitalized and live again.

In the remainder of this chapter are things I learned from the study of the Scriptures and from the strenuous, often painful work of pastoral ministry. I found that the Scriptures are full of helpful data on the subject of church revitalization, but there is a dearth of

Christian literature dealing with the subject. In the light of Scripture and my own pastoral experience, I want to point out certain basic tenets of revitalization, and I place them under two main categories. The first has to do with the prevailing dynamics facing you in a dying church. The second consists of the principles needed to move a church from the throes of death to the celebration of life in Christ.

Prevailing Dynamics in a Dying Church

The dynamics in a dying church are many and varied, and the following are what I believe to be the most basic and prevalent.

Image and Reputation

The longer the church follows a pattern of decline, the worse it is for the public image and reputation of the church. The community at large and the neighboring churches form opinions as to the church's condition. The people who do the most damage to the church's reputation are the ones who have left the church and gone to other communions. Their "inside" information and "horror stories" about the decline of the church, dangers in the neighborhood, and lack of resources in the congregation, do a great deal of harm. I can't tell you how many times I have sat in the home of someone who would not listen to a word I said because of the damaging reports he had heard about our church from previous members. The longer a church remains in decline, the longer the list of evil rumors becomes, and the harder the task of revitalization.

Nostalgia

One of the most destructive dynamics is that of a group of people living in the past. In fact, you will probably find that you were not called with the hope of moving the church forward, but backward, to recapture the "glory days." My response to this expectation was that we were called "to forget what lies behind" and "press on." Specifically, I said, "If yesteryear was so great, why are we in the shape that we find ourselves in today?" It worked, but let me warn you: the river of nostalgia has a sweeping current that takes the church backward and downward to destruction.

Tradition

There is usually an abundance of tradition in old and dying churches. At Pinelands Presbyterian Church, I found a group of fifty people trying to uphold the tradition of 900. You could shoot a cannon filled with grapeshot from front to back and not hit a single person during the morning worship service. Yet some wanted to go to two services in the morning. Why? Because two services were symbolic of the glory days! The logic? Two services will recapture those days.

There is a positive aspect to this. For instance, if you attempt to plant a new church, you will probably start with a core group of twenty-five or so who come from other churches. Many of these are with you because they can't get along anywhere else, and all of them have their own traditions and ideas of what a church ought to be and do. In revitalization at least you have only *one* tradition to face, and it's already proved to be dead.

Another positive note is that unlike the church planter with his twenty-five discontents from other churches who have tenuous commitments to the new work, your fifty are there with you and deeply want to stay. Their reasons may not be entirely valid, but at least they are committed. Your challenge is to channel that commitment from the building and traditions of the church to the person and cause of Christ.

Prepared for Defeat

Not only is the church living in the past (nostalgia) with vague recollections of long ago victories, but even worse, there is an air of defeat and despair about the future. Everything has failed! So the church members will have a well-rehearsed list of reasons as to why whatever you propose, no matter how biblical, is sure to fail. "The neighborhood has changed" . . . "we've tried that and it didn't work" . . . "neighborhood kids will wreck the building" . . . "there isn't money in the budget for that" are just a few on the list. The church has become like a sports team that has lost every game for ten years and already has a list of excuses for the defeats it expects the next season.

Disrepair

Because the organism has not grown, the organization is almost sure to be in disarray. Because attendance at worship and offerings are down, church programs and ministries have been cut and shelved. The cutting probably was done with little thought given to how much particular ministries were needed or what long-range consequences there would be if they were dropped. There was no longer enough money to pay for them, and so the programs were dropped.

Usually the condition of the church building is the public statement of disrepair. The facilities suffer because of the internal financial pressures. At Pinelands this problem had become acute. The transient nature of the neighborhood, coupled with the declining condition of the facilities and grounds, made the church an inviting target for vandalism. Barely a day or night went by without windows being broken, walls painted with obscenities, or outside lights broken.

Let me share a positive thought and a warning about church facilities, buildings, and grounds. In a revitalization pastoral ministry you have the "luxury" of using existing buildings. They are there already, by God's merciful providence, and they only need to be filled. By way of contrast, the planter and organizer of a new church has the problem of finding temporary facilities in which to hold services, and later of buying lands and erecting buildings. That can be a time-consuming distraction from your ministry. Buildings and other church facilities must be viewed as a means to an end, and never the end itself. It probably is easier to keep this in mind in a revitalization ministry than in a church planting situation where you tend to be preoccupied by the need for larger building facilities.

Unrealistic Expectations

The dying church is like a person sick with cancer. Last minute cures are possible, and God can do all things. But if the patient is to recover, the normal course is going to require building the spiritual blocks of the church, layer by layer, beginning with the foundation. Many of the spiritually sensitive and discerning members probably have left the church. Therefore, cultivation of spiritual growth and biblical expectations in the lives of God's people is one of the first challenges facing the revitalization pastor. As much as the members want an "instant" cure, a "quick fix," they must learn to go back to the basics, cultivating a biblical faith, walking with God and thinking His thoughts, loving Jesus Christ and obeying His commands, depending on His grace and Spirit and the power of the gospel.

How do you as a pastor contend with these and the many other dynamics of a dying church? The immediate response by most pastors is usually to speak against these signposts of death from the pulpit. Please resist that temptation. Instead, present the positive teachings of God's Word as to the things Christ can and will do, by grace, when His people are committed and faithful. You as the pastor must lead the congregation out of the doldrums of a dying church to, what I call, the "Principled Dynamics of a Living Church."

Principled Dynamics of a Living Church

Vision

First, it is crucial that you set before the people a positive, clear, and concise biblical vision for the church coming back to life. In order to remove the tendency toward nostalgia (living in the past) and defeatism (dwelling on the disappointments of the past), God's people must be called to action that is faithful to the Word of God. They must also be given the kind of confidence that only the promises of God's Word can provide. Christ has clearly declared, "I will build my church; and the gates of hell shall not prevail against it" (Matt. 16:18, KJV). His people must hear that promise, believe it, and act upon it. "Where there is no vision [revelation], the people perish" (Prov. 29:18, KJV). I know that passage has been misused by church leadership to garner support for pet projects, building programs, and many other things. But the *fact* of the verse is that vision *unifies* and propels God's people forward into positive action for the future instead of dwelling on past victories or defeats. The *demand* of the verse (revelation) is that the vision be biblical in content, scope, and direction. Here are at least some of the contents of a biblical vision for the church.

1. Worship That Is Transforming. In John 4:23, Jesus is recorded as saying that the Father seeks true worshipers who worship Him in spirit and truth. Think of it, the Father seeks our genuine worship qualified by internal enthusiasm (spirit) and formed and instructed by His Word (truth). Worship is the opportunity for praise and reflection on the greatness of the triune God as we meditate on the majesty of His person and the power of His works. Worship that is true worship (called by A. W. Tozer the "mission crown jewel" in Christianity) is done by the transformed and is at the same time transforming.

2. Discipleship at Several Levels. There are two dynamics to discipleship. The first has to do with what should be happening in you. As a pastor to the congregation, your own spiritual health, growth, and vitality are crucial to the whole process of revitalizing the congregation.

Second, you need to look at the plan that Paul, under divine inspiration, gave Timothy for the revitalization of the church at Ephesus.

Let's look at the pastor-congregation principle laid down in II Timothy 2:2, bearing in mind also the model of Christ's work with His disciples. The Scripture speaks of three levels of discipling, and they begin with you the pastor. "The things which you have heard me say in the presence of many witnesses, entrust to reliable men, who will also be qualified to teach others" (II Tim. 2:2). Upon closer examination the three levels of discipling look like this:

Level 1. Paul (mature mentor) to Timothy
(maturing pastor)

Level 2. Timothy (maturing pastor) to
faithful men (proven leaders)

Level 3. Faithful men (proven leaders)
to others (potential leaders)

Get the picture? The implication is that you need to be discipled just like Timothy. You must find a Paul and keep learning. Once you quit learning you have disqualified yourself as a teacher, because disciplers are first and foremost learners.

Let me illustrate this. In order to follow this principle in my own pastoral ministry at Pinelands one of the first things I did was to seek out the pastors in the area whom the Lord was obviously blessing in rich ways. In my search for such pastors, I did not limit the field to my own denomination, the Presbyterian Church in America. As I sat down with those men and asked them to share with me what they believed were the ways God was blessing their ministries, I took great pains to assure them they could speak freely. I was there to learn from them, not criticize them. After listening to the ministry stories of a great many men, I focused on two men who freely shared their hearts with me and challenged me personally and pastorally. I remain thankful to this day for the wisdom and love, which is always spelled T-I-M-E, that these men offered me.

The second step you must take is to find faithful men, proven leaders, through whom you can multiply your ministry. Your goal is to *multiply* followers of Christ through your church and not just add members one by one. The third step is to make the discipleship process go full circle by challenging these leaders with whom you're working in special ways to disciple others. These others are potential leaders whom you may seek to identify together.

Concerning your personal discipling ministry, it ought to have four levels occurring simultaneously as you follow Christ's model and Paul's exhortation to Timothy:

> Christ (You)—multitude (your large group/
> congregation), i.e., public
> ministry of the Word
>
> Christ (You)—twelve (your small group of
> potential leaders)
>
> Christ (You)—three, i.e., Peter, James,
> John (smaller groups of your
> proven leaders)
>
> Christ (You)—one, i.e., John, the disciple
> whom He loved (your account-
> ability partner)

Because of the influence of the Navigators, many people think "one-to-one" as soon as they hear the word discipleship. While I praise God that the Navigators have kept the discipleship principle alive, I personally believe most discipleship takes place in the group context, and the one-to-one relationship is more of an accountability arrangement.

Look back at the II Timothy 2:2 passage. Paul discipled Timothy in a group, "in the presence of many witnesses." Timothy was to disciple faithful "men" (plural). They in turn discipled "others" (plural). I realize that the size of your group or congregation may not be large to begin with, but you have to start somewhere. Then comes the small group of *potential* leaders followed by an even smaller group of *proven* leaders. Then begin a one-to-one account-ability relationship with a key individual, inside or outside your church, whom you can trust and from whom you can learn. Above all be willing to learn, for in a revitalization ministry encouragement and instruction are two inputs you will need in abundance. Like David, find your Jonathan.

The beauty of discipleship is that it builds balance into the church ministry. True discipleship demands that the discipler do three things. He must evangelize (win the disciple), equip (train the disciple), exhort (send the disciple) to reproduce so that he becomes involved in evangelizing, equipping, and exhorting. Result? Repro-duction by multiplication instead of addition.

Another blessing is that by your leadership model of discipleship the church becomes multi-dimensional instead of one dimensional. So many churches concentrate just on evangelizing or equipping. Discipling promotes a well-rounded, multi-faceted church that wins converts and trains them. And the kind of training they receive pushes them to repeat the process as they grow in grace.

3. *Growth Mentality That Is Biblical.* Church growth as it is de-scribed in Scripture is best explained by a three-tiered formula. It begins with *spiritual* growth, which then leads to *functional* growth, which in turn leads to *statistical* growth. Statistical growth is a direct result of functional growth.

We all know what statistical growth is. It's the "bottom line" everyone looks at when evaluating a church and its effectiveness. But what is functional growth? Simply stated, it is God's people doing what the Bible requires of those who have been made "dis-ciples." They have become *"doers of the Word."* They preach the gospel, they love the brethren, and they are busy doing all the hundreds of other things the Bible talks about as functions that mark genuine disciples of Jesus.

How does that happen? Functional growth is a result of spiritual growth. Spiritual growth is the Word of God being loved, learned, and obeyed by the power of the Holy Spirit for the glory of God in the lives of God's people under the lordship of Christ. Dying churches are identified by the lack of statistical growth. But the real problem is the lack of either functional growth or spiritual growth, or both. Don't put a Band-Aid on the sore spot of statistical stagnation with special programs or hype designed to create numbers, nickels, and noise. Go directly to the infection. Programs cannot create *real* growth. Ministry programs accommodate and/or direct functional growth. The basic issue is whether the church is functioning (obeying the Word of God) or is failing to mature spiritually (quenching or grieving the Spirit of God).

The biblical vision for the growth of the church includes the three-tiered view of growth, and one of your earliest tasks as a revitalization leader is to get the congregation to see that the lack of statistical growth is only a symptom. The root cause lies in the church's spiritual stagnation and functional breakdown. If the root cause is removed, the symptoms most likely will change.

4. Breaking Down Jealous Criticism of Other Churches. Dying churches become cynical and critical, especially if there are other churches nearby that are faring better. It is difficult for a dying church to explain to itself its own condition, and the tendency is to find something wrong with those churches which appear to be growing. If other churches are growing, something must be wrong with their doctrine. Their leaders must be "show people," and their strategy for gaining members lacks integrity. Some members of dying churches develop an attitude that assumes that if you are faithful to God's Word you are consigned to be a "remnant," a "holy huddle." A critical spirit soon eats you, your ministry, and the church. To combat this tendency at the two churches I helped to revitalize, we privately and publicly prayed for the continued success of other evangelical churches in the community and thanked God for them.

5. *Transformation at the Deepest Level of Homogeneity.* In the part of Miami where Pinelands Church ministered, tremendous social upheaval was taking place. Foreign immigration, legal and illegal, was producing traumatic social and cultural changes. In our neighborhood, church growth experts said there was no settled homogeneous principle from which to work, and therefore the church needed to relocate. They were right and they were wrong: right in that racially, economically, socially, and culturally the neighborhood was totally diverse—it was a real hodgepodge of people groups—but wrong in that there was in fact a principle of homogeneity. They were all sinners, and if Christ called them, He would "break down the dividing wall."

Why not have a congregation unified in diversity through the grace of God? This vision consumed us.

I believe the homogeneous principle taught in church growth books does work, and I also believe that in many cases it is used as a cop-out. The only legitimate obstacle that by necessity will divide a congregation committed to Christ and His Word is diversity in language. Our vision at Pinelands was for a multi-cultural, multi-racial, and economically diverse congregation. And by God's grace, it happened. After three years you could feel the excitement when you stood in the packed sanctuary containing people, one-third of whom were black, representing over twenty nationalities, some of them rich, some of them poor, and all of them holding hands and singing, "I'm So Glad I'm a Part of the Family of God." I have seen the Savior take those "who were not a people" and make them "the people of God," cutting across social barriers as nobody outside the kingdom would ever believed could happen.

Transfer growth is not what a church should aim for when it is seeking revitalization. Transfer growth will come spontaneously in most cases where the church is alive and vigorous, for there aren't many such churches around. In the average community, if a church is experiencing the power of Christ's resurrection life, people will come. They will transfer their membership because they are hungry for a true Word from God on Sunday and a fellowship where love and truth flow together in the power of the Holy Spirit. Biological growth, covenantal evangelism, will happen because the church families are spiritually healthy and godly parents are faithful to their covenant vows on behalf of their offspring. God honors such families with His work of grace in their children, and the churches prosper as a result

But the major goal of the church seeking and experiencing revitalization must be conversion growth. Because when people are being rescued from the kingdom of darkness and incorporated into the kingdom of light through the church's ministry, a power is unleashed that melts old differences and breaks down barriers. Nothing in the church or the community is ever the same again, for you have realized transformation at the deepest levels of homogeneity.

Image

The second principle of revitalization has to do with the church's image, its name and reputation in the community. A church gets its image in one of four ways: (1) The community gives it to you. ("Oh, that's the church that doesn't . . ." or "that's the church that believes. . . .") (2) Other churches assign you a place in the circle of ecclesiastical bodies. Churches put each other in certain categories just like people do to each other. (3) You will haphazardly develop an image through careless decisions, bad publicity (gossip), and poor leadership. Many a church has to live with its past, the mistakes and narrowness of former generations. (4) Or you will choose an image for yourself! And that option offers hope for churches eager for revitalization.

Image is the communication of your biblical vision for the church to its members and, through their lives and the ministries of the church, to the world.

Whenever you produce a publication, whether a church bulletin or a brochure, do it right. I'm not talking about extravagance or opulence, but *excellence*. Break the chain of mediocrity and make excellence a characteristic everyone who comes to your services and participates in your ministries can expect.

If possible, change the church name if that is what it takes to communicate your new vision and project a new image. In Charlotte, to communicate our dedication to a Christ-centered ministry, we chose an appropriate church name (Christ Covenant) and a church verse (Col. 1:18—"that in all things Christ might have the preeminence" [KJV]). In order to announce to the community our intention to glorify God by developing a balanced ministry through discipleship, a church motto was needed. We chose the motto, "Developing Disciples for God's Glory." The church's name, verse, and motto are placed on everything we publish, and we verbally communicate what they mean whenever possible. We repeat them to ourselves, we announce them to the community, and most of all we seek to make them real in substance and not just symbols.

Pulpit Ministry

I could say much more about revitalization. On the topic of the power of prayer, it would take chapters to tell you how the Lord has answered the prayers of His people for leaders, land, new converts, and growing ministries. But I am going to conclude this chapter by focusing on where I believe the battle for revitalization is won or lost. It is the pulpit ministry of the pastor-teacher. Where a man of God, called and gifted to explain the Word of God, protects his life and schedule in order to prepare faithful biblical expositions that issue forth with loving application so that sin is exposed and Christ is exalted, God blesses that ministry with newness of life.

As I visited a number of successful churches, I noticed two things. First, each successful church has a *distinctive* that usually comes from the strengths of the leaders and their biblical convictions about the church and its mandate. Some churches are noted for evangelism, others discipleship, still others small groups. But each successful church has one particular thing that it does especially well and that sets it apart from the others.

The second thing that I noticed is that every growing church without exception has a better-than-average pulpit ministry. Spurgeon said that the Thermopylae of Christianity is the pulpit, and I believe him. More than that, I believe the Scriptures: "Faith cometh from hearing and hearing from the Word of Christ" (Rom. 10:17, KJV). We are saved "through the foolishness of the message preached" (I Cor. 1:21, NASB).

People won't come miles or even blocks every Sunday unless they can be sure they will hear something good. Fancy bulletins and innovative worship services cannot sustain life and growth. Only the Word of God preached in the "demonstration and power of the Holy Spirit," proclaiming "Christ and him crucified," can keep life in the church. The towns and cities of America are littered with churches that forget this, and that is why so many need revitalization. A strong biblical pulpit must be restored and maintained if life, once restored, is to continue.

The Pastor's Perspective on the Church and Commitment to Evangelism

Perspectives are crucial to a revitalization pastor: his perspective on the power of the preached Word, the importance of the family, the place of prayer, the nature of leadership, and many others. But one of the most crucial factors is his perspective on the congregation, his commitment to them, and his desire for their future participation in the revitalized church.

I have seen two very different perspectives on the congregation among the pastors of revitalization projects. Some view their inherited congregation as a "scaffold" upon which they must stand to build the new work. The older members are seen as an expendable entity. If they become part of the new work, fine. But those who do not fit into the new work are, like scaffolds, dismantled and cast aside.

I consider the "scaffold" perspective a callous misuse of Christ's church. It operates on the pragmatic principle that the end justifies the means. But the fact is that the means determine the end. The older members need pastoral care. They have been wounded and discouraged as they have watched their church weaken and come near to dying. Their spiritual needs have not always been met as the church limped along. What they need least of all now is a pastor who manipulates them for some "higher ends" he has in mind. Their souls, too, are precious in God's sight, and as you are their pastor, they are your first responsibility. *The pastor's relationship with the existing congregation, however weak or small, sets the tone, the pace, and the environment for everything else he hopes will happen.*

The perspective I recommend is one in which the inherited congregation is viewed as the "foundation" of the potential congregation. These people are not leftovers but a flock of God suffering and in need of the healing touch of a shepherd. The integrity of the pastor in dealing lovingly with those whom the Lord has granted him will be the determining factor for both the quality and quantity of the future congregation that he hopes will emerge.

The first part of my ministry of revitalization at Pinelands was not spent in advertising, neighborhood canvassing, or new program implementation. I began by first visiting the families of the existing congregation, accompanied by an elder. For many it was the first time in years a pastor or elder had been in their homes on a ministerial visit. In fact, one family told me it was the first time in twenty-two years that a pastor had been in their home. Is there any wonder the church was dying?

Another important thing to do is to contact those who have fallen away from the church. My first three months at Pinelands were spent visiting the existing congregation, and later I went looking for the hundred members who were on the books but unaccounted for. The parable of the shepherd seeking the one that was lost took on new meaning as ten of the 100 either were converted or rededicated their lives to Christ. Two other families in the middle of divorce proceedings were reconciled through a renewed commitment to Christ and His Word as a result of my visits.

The bottom line is that in three years we went from an average attendance of fifty to over 300. More than half of those added were by conversion or rededication to Christ. But almost as gratifying as the conversion growth was that only one family from the original congregation was lost to another communion in the process of revitalization. Instead of feeling disenfranchised or being dismantled, the former members became a vital part of the "new work"of the Lord in Pinelands, rejoicing in what the Lord was doing and with a vested interest in the church's ministry and the new vision for the community we served.

Finally, a biblical vision for the church must not merely include evangelism as one program among many. The evangelistic dimension must be emphasized in everything the church does. Evangelism is not supplemental. It is *fundamental* to revitalization.

At Christ Covenant Church, where I now serve, we have a training program called Lifestyle Evangelism and Discipleship (L.E.A.D.), and it is vital to our outreach in the community. Another program is called Fisherman Bible Fellowship, in which members conduct Bible studies in homes and offices during the day. But programs as such don't make evangelism, nor do they make a church evangelistic. Evangelism programs only serve to train those already alive with the gospel and sharing their faith, who want to do so in a more organized and effective way.

Evangelism is contagious once it starts happening in a congregation. Conversions have an impact not only on the people brought to Christ but also on the entire congregation. Nothing turns the tide toward revitalization faster than genuine conversions, and when they happen right within the traditional membership, they have an additional impact. I will illustrate this.

The first sermon I preached at Pinelands was on saving faith. I closed the message in prayer and the organist-choir director was supposed to play. But she didn't. I was panic-stricken! My first Sunday. I knew Satan was attacking. I opened one eye and glanced sternly over toward the organ. She wasn't there! Now real panic set in! Then I heard sobbing, and I looked beneath the pulpit. There she was. I had not even given an invitation, but the Lord had caused His Word to move her to confess Christ publicly. The choir director-organist for eight years at Pinelands Church was brought from death to life. Her words were simple, "I'm here to become a Christian."

A holy excitement began to grip our "throng" of forty people. That week a deacon named Jack came to me and said, "Pastor, last Sunday I wanted to come forward also. I'm not a Christian. The only reason I didn't is that I did not want to embarass you since I'm a church officer." My reply to Jack was twofold. First, your coming to Christ will never be an embarassment. And second, you don't need to come forward after a sermon. You can give your life to Christ right now. Praise God he did! Then he asked me to give an invitation the next Sunday because he wanted to acknowledge Christ publicly. His own words were that he had been living a lie for fourteen years, and he needed to make it right publicly in front of the Lord and the people of God.

I promised him I would give an invitation next Sunday morning. On Thursday of that week, Jack almost severed his thumb with a power saw at work. Using microsurgery, they sewed it on and told him to rest in bed with his arm up for weeks. The next Sunday, to my surprise, Jack was in the worship service. I gave an invitation, not really expecting anything since Jack was in such pain. His whole arm wrapped like a mummy extended in the air, and his thumb was actually held in place with a button on the thumb nail. He came forward, but not alone. Along with him came his wife, *and* the chairman of the diaconate with his wife, followed by two elders with their wives. Jack's free arm went around me, and he whispered in my ear, "Harry, Satan could have cut my arm off, and I would be standing here today."

I decided to give an invitation the next week without being asked. Twenty-six people came forward to publicly confess Christ as Lord and Savior. Revitalization! The gospel was at work by the power of God's Spirit.

It is no surprise that three years later Jack has become an effective elder, and the church is reaching out evangelistically to a diverse community that would chase most church growth experts away. Morning and evening services are full largely with new believers. And a multi-racial, multi-cultural church is alive and growing on a dead-end street in Miami, Florida, for the glory of God.

Revitalization ministry? It's a challenge . . . a privilege . . . an adventure . . . and most of all, an opportunity for Christ's gospel to be revealed for what it is, the power of God unto salvation in a world of many diverse peoples.

__ 14 __

Pastor-Evangelists:
Need of the Hour Everywhere
Roger S. Greenway

At the meetings of the Consultation on World Evangelization held in Thailand in 1980, George Peters, who for many years taught Missions at Dallas Theological Seminary, made several pointed comments about pastors and evangelism. He talked about the churches of Europe, where in his retirement Peters made annual visits addressing pastors and furloughing missionaries. Peters told us that he had recently addressed a gathering of 350 European pastors, all of them conservative in their theology. He asked them how many had ever studied evangelism. Only five said that they had taken a course in the subject. Twenty had attended at least a one-day workshop in evangelism. The vast majority had never received any formal instruction on how to do or organize evangelism. Was there any connection, Peters asked, between this lack of training and the major complaint throughout Europe that the churches weren't growing? His own analysis was that the "European churches and their leaders have never seen the connection between evangelism and pastoral ministry."

My own observations in other parts of the world bear out what George Peters said. When churches fail to present the claims of Christ evangelistically to the unsaved world, a series of things happen. The gospel of God's saving grace no longer glows in pulpit and pew as it formerly did, and members slip away. Among the remnant, religious energies are directed toward other things, usually social issues and human development. Theologians add to the process by providing a conceptual framework of soteriological universalism that does not require personal conversion and thereby excludes biblical evangelism. Evangelism, in fact, is redefined as social action. As far as the churches are concerned, it is a downward spiral as unevangelistic leaders produce unevangelistic institutions, which in turn produce a body of people whose religious impulses go in many directions, carrying some of them even to distant parts of the world, doing many commendable things but lacking evangelistic motivation and power. Such workers cannot produce growing churches. Though pastors are not the whole problem, they certainly are a key part of it. And, I would add, they can also be the catalysts who turn the spiral around.

George Peters made a second statement about the strategy mission agencies follow around the world: "I've just come back from a round-the-world tour of mission fields on behalf of several major boards, and I'm disgusted. I've seen a thousand small, stagnant churches that aren't going anywhere. I told the mission executives they had better stop emphasizing church planting until they've learned to make churches grow. The pastors don't know how to evangelize and the churches just hang on with a handful of members."

One of the dismal realities we don't talk about in mission literature, particularly literature of a promotional kind, is that we have planted a lot of churches that are as evangelistically sterile as many of our older churches in the West. Nongrowing churches in places where receptivity to the gospel is generally high is an unresolved dilemma, and I believe God has raised up the pentecostal churches partly as an indictment of the older denominations. The evangelistic sterility of mainline churches, including some that remain orthodox in their doctrine, is a terrible witness to Christianity and in my opinion stands at the top of the list of the problems we face in world evangelization.

My thesis is that the solution begins with the pastors who lead the congregations and the training they receive for ministry. Many years ago, the great missionary statesman John R. Mott expressed this truth succinctly:

> The secret of enabling the church to press forward in the non-Christian world is one of leadership. The people do not go

beyond their leaders in knowledge and zeal, nor surpass them in consecration and sacrifice. The Christian pastor . . . holds the divinely appointed office for inspiring and guiding the thought and activities of the church. By virtue of his position he can be a mighty force in the world's evangelization.

In the first chapter of this book I said that the pastor's responsibility in regard to evangelism is threefold. He must teach and preach evangelism from the Word of God, building a solid basis of understanding and commitment within the congregation. He must model evangelism in his own life and ministry, teaching by example and guiding others in the process. Finally, the pastor must mobilize the membership in ways that put feet to doctrine and theory. His role is that of organizer, equipper, and catalyst. Under his leadership the members explore new possibilities for reaching their community and incorporate evangelism into every department of church life.

Much of the book has dealt with ways this can be done, and my purpose in this final chapter is to highlight certain issues and review the general framework of pastoral evangelism. I include a number of illustrations of pastoral evangelism in action, building around the three pivotal areas of modeling, teaching, and organizing. In response to the possible accusation that I have been unduly hard on pastors, I begin with some thoughts in their defense, things that need to be said though they imply a degree of admonishment.

In Defense of the Average Pastor

First, something needs to be said about para-church organizations that specialize in evangelism and whose record in gaining converts frequently exceeds that of the established church. At the Consultation in Thailand, I heard pastors from various parts of the world complain that they felt they were being victimized in the eyes of their people. Pastors, they complained, always get the blame when the church compares poorly with highly charged efforts of para-church mission agencies. Often the members themselves, or the circumstances in which the church is located and working, inhibit the kind of growth people demand. The pastors gathered in Thailand pointed out also that para-church organizations generally are structured differently from the church. Their main intent is missionary service and outreach, whereas pastors and churches have a host of additional responsibilities besides evangelism. Workers in para-church mission agencies generally don't have to counsel troubled families, conduct funerals, teach ladies societies, and comfort the sick and elderly. They can focus on the purpose for which they are organized and maintained, evangelism. If their success in that department seems to exceed that of the average pastor and the institutional church, the reasons are obvious.

The pastors' complaint is legitimate, and critics of the church need to be reminded that the ministries of the church go far beyond the specialized concerns of para-church organizations. They must remember, too, that the task of evangelism is not completed when people become believers. Discipleship is a long ongoing process, involving years of instruction, guidance, and discipline. Without churches to do this, what would become of the fruits of the para-church activities? The need, as I see it, is for church and para-church institutions to work together more closely, to integrate their efforts and avoid all semblance of competition and leadership stealing. *I maintain the conviction that, when the local church enjoys the leadership of pastors committed to evangelism, it takes a back seat to no other organization in drawing sinners to Christ and nurturing them over the long haul to faithful and responsible discipleship.*

Second, I defend those pastors who serve in difficult locations. There are rural communities where many residents have departed and few young people stay around. Pastors in declining communities see many of the talented people leaving, and they easily become frustrated and discouraged because all the exciting places of ministry seem to be somewhere else. Then there are inner city neighborhoods where people's lives are, in varying degrees, shattered and torn apart by sin and its consequences. Numerical growth is slow, and pastors spend much of their time healing wounds and holding members together against a withering barrage of negative forces. Some churches are located in places where they are cut off from the mainstream because of language or cultural differences, and yet the remnant is there and requires pastoral care.

Highly favorable locations can also be deceptive. There are communities so favorable that almost any church will grow, even without evangelism. In North America and Europe these usually are suburban locations where large numbers of middle-class families are moving in and can be counted on to join an evangelical church. Church planters rely heavily on demographic studies to determine where these high potential locations are likely to develop, and they shape their strategy accordingly. From a practical standpoint this makes sense, and many of the highly acclaimed churches in America are built in this way. But the strategy, especially if it is followed to the exclusion of all others, has some serious drawbacks. It may represent the planned neglect of urban neighborhoods where large numbers of people need to be evangelized and pastored. It tends to focus entirely on "our kind" of people, to the neglect of social and ethnic minorities. It may say in effect that the only churches worth planting and pastoring are those which promise, in businessmen's fashion, a "high return" on the investment. Therefore, in defense of some "low yield" pastorates I raise this word of caution. *God's people are found in many different locations and circumstances, and all of them need mission-hearted pastors. Heaven will reward many who receive no laurels on earth. Let us not look down on those less-fertile fields, but honor the laborers for their perseverance.*

Third, in defense of pastors who feel frustrated over evangelism something needs to be said about the Christian colleges and seminaries that fail to provide adequate training in this area. What George Peters observed in the case of European-educated pastors is also true of schooling on this side of the Atlantic and in many Third World institutions. Most courses in missions and evangelism are heavy on theory but terribly light on practice, and some graduates have never studied evangelism at all. Courses in the department of practical theology traditionally are oriented toward the internal needs of congregations and not toward the evangelization of the unsaved outside. It is no wonder, therefore, that pastors feel frustrated when churches decline and evangelism-minded lay people look elsewhere for direction. *Evangelism tends to have the same importance and place in the churches that it has in the seminaries, and for that reason our concern for evangelism through local churches carries us to the schools where church leadership is formed.*

Few people have known more about seminaries around the world and how well they succeed in producing pastor-evangelists than James F. Hopewell, associated as he was with the Theological Education Fund from its beginning in 1958, long before it had formal connection with the World Council of Churches and its viewpoint. Hopewell visited hundreds of theological institutions around the world with the specific purpose of cutting through the outer, superficial appearances and getting at the core of their mission and ministry. Defining "mission" as the witness Christians make outside the normal frontiers of the church, and "candidate" as the person being prepared by some theological institution for a career in Christian service, Hopewell said the following:

> The problem is that surprisingly few candidates are prepared to engage in that mission with any consistency or accuracy. And while this fault may be attributed to most any aspect of modern church structure, it seems particularly encouraged by the pattern of theological education now practiced in most seminaries around the world. . . .
>
> Now I would like to contend . . . that most of these factors that comprise our understanding of typical theological education have been unconsciously designed to avoid, and therefore to hinder, the basic Christian intention of mission. And I do not mean to beat the anti-intellectual drum against higher learning. What rather concerns an increasing number of critics is that the very tool of higher learning has been misappropriated to perform a third-rate job for a second-rate church structure. In a time when our understanding of the ministry more and more implies its dynamic, missionary function, we continue to rely upon a system of preparation which at its roots is essentially static and isolationist.[1]

In view of the increased pressure building up today for leadership that knows how to evangelize, I predict that Christian colleges and seminaries will have to revamp their programs or face decline. The realities of a world in which the percentage of unchurched and unsaved people rises every year demand that church leadership be

1. James F. Hopewell, "Preparing the Candidate for Mission," *International Review of Missions* 56:158-63.

trained in new ways to meet the challenge. *Evangelism must be returned to its rightful place in the classroom and in the church, or the trend toward para-churchism will become a stampede.*

Certain readers may want to challenge this, and therefore I invite them to reflect on the following. A well-known evangelical seminary that has always stood for scholarship and doctrinal conservatism recently sent a questionnaire to its alumni asking them to rank the courses they felt had been the most helpful in preparing them for pastoral ministry. As reported by the pastors, the top five were church history, Greek, Hebrew, systematics, and biblical theology. At or near the bottom were preaching, evangelism, and church growth. Another questionnaire was sent to the elders and lay leaders of the churches being served by the seminary's graduates. They were asked to indicate the chief *weaknesses* they observed in pastors. Surprise! The top three weaknesses were in communication, preaching, and evangelism, areas that lie at the exact opposite of the "most helpful" courses identified by the pastors. That seminary, and many similar institutions, really has something to think about. The discrepancy in responses may reflect the quality of the teaching in the respective departments. In addition, it reflects a profound difference of perception between scholars and church members as to what people in the pew are looking for in their leaders. Certainly the members had detected certain deficiencies in the training received by their pastors, and they were outspoken in their desire to see the gaps filled. That particular seminary is taking serious steps to shore up its weaknesses, and I hope all pastor-training institutions will take warning.

Areas in Which Pastors Preach and Teach Evangelism

Responsibility for equipping members for kingdom service and evangelism lies with the pastors, the spiritual leaders of God's people. The biblical pattern is teaching, modeling, and organizing. In teaching I include Sunday preaching, which in most churches is the chief didactic instrument. Unless the pastor's teaching-preaching sounds forth the gospel and creates the atmosphere of evangelism in the church, it is unlikely that the church will become mobilized for effective outreach.

Members must be able to expect that in every worship service the good news of hope and salvation through Christ will be heard in such a manner that children, youth, and the casual visitor will be able to grasp something of its meaning. Unfortunately, this is not the case in every church. Some time ago I was talking with an elder from a large Reformed congregation. I know the pastor of that church well, and he is a gifted speaker and deeply committed to the orthodox expression of the faith. The elder, a man of long-standing leadership in the church, related to me how he and his wife had witnessed by word and deed for many years to his unchurched neighbors. Repeatedly they had invited the couple to attend church, but they had always refused. Finally, they agreed to go just once. "My wife and I took them to the pentecostal church," said the elder. Surprised, I asked him why they had not taken them to their own church. "Well, you know how it is in our church," he replied. "Our preacher is great, but he's usually very deep, and we were afraid they wouldn't hear the gospel."

That was an awful indictment on the elder's church and its pulpit ministry. It sheds light also on the fact that that particular church has sent scores of members into para-church ministries, all of them perfectly legitimate in themselves but not contributing in any direct way to the growth of the congregation. Various attempts over the years were made by the church to develop an effective outreach program, but nothing seemed to work. The church kept nourishing the faith of its members, many of whom went off to engage in evangelistic ministries through outside organizations, while the church hardly drew a new member except through its own children, occasional transfers, and a few marriages.

The preaching of sound doctrine without a burning heart for evangelism is as unbiblical as it is dangerous. Likewise are pastoral prayers without tears for lost souls. The evangelistic tone of the congregation is set on Sunday where the passion of the pastor's heart becomes evident and is transmitted to the members. In a sermon entitled "Without Christ—Nothing" Charles H. Spurgeon said the following:

> You may have sound doctrine, and yet do nothing unless you have Christ *in your spirit*. I have known all the doctrines of grace

to be unmistakably preached, and yet there have been no conversions; for this reason, that they were not expected and scarcely desired. In former years many orthodox preachers thought it to be their sole duty to comfort and confirm the godly few who by dint of great perseverance found out the holes and corners in which they prophesied. These brethren spoke of sinners as of people whom God might possibly gather in if he thought fit to do so; but they did not care much whether he did so or not. As to weeping over sinners as Christ wept over Jerusalem; as to venturing to invite them to Christ as the Lord did when he stretched out his hands all the day long; as to lamenting with Jeremiah over a perishing people, they had n sympathy with such emotions and feared that they savoured of Arminianism. Both preacher and congregation were cased in a hard shell, and lived as if their own salvation was the sole design of their existence. If anybody did grow zealous and seek conversions, straightway they said he was indiscreet, or conceited. When a church falls into this condition it is, as to its spirit, "without Christ." What comes of it? Some of you know by your own observation what does come of it. The comfortable corporation exists and grows for a little while, but it comes to nothing in the long run; and so it must: there can be no fruit-bearing where there is not the spirit of Christ as well as the doctrine of Christ. Except the spirit of the Lord rest upon you, causing you to agonize for the salvation of men even as Jesus did, ye can do nothing.[2]

Spurgeon spoke directly to the point, and the only corrective for the "comfortable corporation" is to be led by pastors who have the heart of the Great Pastor, Jesus. His heart must increasingly become ours so that His ministry may shine through us. Preachers and churches without Christ's spirit of compassion for the lost have always been around. They display certain strengths for a while, even a long while, but eventually they divide, dwindle, and close down unless they repent and return to the spirit of the Lord. In our day we see how thousands of renewed Christians spend their energies on ministries apart from the organized churches mainly because of this condition.

2. Charles H. Spurgeon, *Sermons on Revival* (Grand Rapids: Zondervan, 1958), pp. 187-88.

Worship and preaching stand at the core of congregational life. Whenever churches have growth problems, you can be certain something is wrong with their worship life. On the other hand, preaching that is biblical, intelligible, winsome, and delivered in the power of the Holy Spirit sets churches on fire and sends members into the streets charged with enthusiasm to draw others in.

Lyle E. Schaller, whose writings about the church and the ministry every pastor should devour, has given what he calls the "Seven Earmarks of Growing Churches." In an article that appeared in *Second Monday*, May 1981, Schaller says that churches that grow successfully through evangelism are characterized by the following elements, which I have slightly recast:

1. *Biblical Preaching.* To the surprise of many church members, says Schaller, more people on the outside are looking for good biblical preaching than we generally assume. They will come to a church where the preacher delivers an authentic word from the Lord and applies Scripture to the real needs of today. I will say more about this point later.

2. *Emphasis on Evangelism.* In growing churches, evangelism is not left for the pastor or a few "mission enthusiasts." Such churches have a cadre of unpaid lay evangelists who are motivated by what they hear from the pulpit to go out and win others to Christ.

3. *Strong Emphasis on Fellowship.* Whereas in most traditional churches the membership circle is larger than the fellowship circle because a percentage of members do not get involved and never become active, the growing churches have a fellowship circle that is larger than the membership circle. Outsiders are continually being drawn toward Christ and His church by the services and activities of the congregation.

4. *Opportunites to Express Commitment.* Schaller says that growing churches recognize that different people have different gifts and different needs, and these churches intentionally present a wide variety of opportunities for members to affirm their faith, even in its early stages, and express their commitment through the church. When churches have only narrow programs and stifle creative ex-

pression, the gifts and talents of many members remain unused, or people go elsewhere to express their commitment. Such churches neither meet needs nor grow.

5. *Openness to New Leadership.* Growing churches take advantage of new leaders that come into the fellowship from outside the original "church family." Nongrowing churches, however, keep the key leadership positions for people belonging to the "mainline families" that have run the church for a generation or more. A high percentage of churches fall into this category.

6. *Specialties in Ministry.* Churches that continue to draw newcomers into their fellowship are churches that, in addition to the basic ministries found in all congregations, focus on special ministries for which they become well known. These ministries are person-centered, are designed to meet particular needs, intentionally include an evangelistic dimension, and offer church members fresh opportunities to express their gifts and interests.

7. *A Pastor Who Likes People.* Surprisingly enough, not all pastors like people, and it shows. Some pastors prefer books and the solitude of their private studies to the topsy-turvy world of interpersonal relationships and bleeding people. They may be highly trained and skilled in professional ways, but they lack the essential ingredient of love for people.

I was called in once by the pastor of a large Presbyterian church in Mexico City to help him assess what was wrong in the Sunday school. The Sunday school director was highly educated, a professor in the denominational seminary, and he seemed to have everything organized very well. In fact, he took his position in the Sunday school very seriously and chose the best curriculum. After a long talk with him, however, I discovered what the problem was. He realized it himself, and admitted, "I love organizing and directing the Sunday school, but I hate kids." The pupils felt it, the teachers chafed under his leadership, and the whole program suffered. I wonder how many stagnant churches suffer from the same problem.

Returning to point one of Schaller's list of growth characteristics, we note that quality biblical preaching is absolutely essential.

Preaching and Sunday worship set the tone for the whole life of the congregation. What happens on Sunday is the key. Here the character of the church is formed, directions are set, visions are shared, and the Spirit through the Word moves the church in one direction or another. Romans 10:17, a text that years ago I chose as the theme text of my pastoral and missionary ministry, is the clue to it all: "Faith comes from hearing the message, and the message is heard through the word of Christ." Good biblical preaching builds Christians and makes churches grow, and this is the pastor's foremost task. Edgar Whitaker Work expressed it this way:

> Courage in the ministry is a contagious spirit felt by others. When men preach in this spirit their preaching has a power of appeal that grips souls. You catch it in the way they use the Bible. You feel the strong word of truth coming to you as you listen to sermons of this kind. Circumlocutions give way. Direct, positive ways of speech take their place. Plain, simple, straightforward utterance in the Gospel wins attention. Men feel the ribs and structure of the Gospel. Again and again the preacher who is bold and outspoken in these ways makes irresistible use of his text. He thrusts it, as it were, beyond the mind, into the heart. He gives it imperative force with his hearers. They *must* hear, he will not let them close their ears.[3]

Modeling—Test of the Preacher's Grit and Integrity

Good preaching, however, does not stand alone. It must be in combination with the whole ministry of the pastor and the life of the church. This principle has been reiterated in various ways throughout the book.

Vincent Taylor once said that the test of any theologian is, Can he write a tract? Taylor was not interested in any kind of theology that did not help to evangelize. I would add another question: Can the titan in the pulpit lead one soul, in private, to Christ? It is one thing to deliver a fine sermon, and still another to take the message to the street, the sick room, and the house of mourning. These occasions occur over and over again in the normal routine of pastoring, and it

---

3. Edgar Whitaker Work, *Every Minister His Own Evangelist* (Fleming, 1927), p. 125.

is in these day-by-day situations that the pastor becomes the model for the congregation. The members can be depended on to take notice.

Pastoral visitation, particularly in homes and hospitals, is a key to success in ministry and evangelism. When churches become stagnant and membership drops off, it is usually the case that the pastors and the elders have not been calling on the people. When it comes to visitation, there is little difference between the work of the local pastor and the work of the home or foreign missionary. Both require aggressive pursuit of people. A Presbyterian pastor in Canada told me recently what had happened in one of the large churches in Toronto. "The pastors didn't think visiting was part of their job," he said. "They didn't even visit the families of the Kirk session, and as a result the elders didn't visit either. The ministers had the idea that if members needed help, they'd come on their own, and the minister didn't have to go out looking for them." The church he was describing was once one of Toronto's finest, but today it stands almost empty.

Visitation evangelism is one of the great needs of the hour. Some sixty million people in this country are classified as "unchurched." That is, they are not members of a church, nor have they attended religious services for a six-month period except for religious holidays. Many of them are not hostile to the Christian religion, and they show interest in religious subjects. They buy many religious books, including the Bible. What keeps them from joining the community of active believers? One basic reason is that they have not been personally invited to do so. Many pastors and congregations are neglecting the fundamental step of going out after people and inviting them to attend the place of worship. Coupled with this is the need for evidence of pastoral concern and availability. Unchurched people generally have notions about organized religion and about clergymen in particular, which can only be dismissed through pastoral visitation. Pastors need to seek out every possible opportunity to talk to unchurched people about spiritual matters and dispel by personal word and example the false notions outsiders have about churches. In actuality, pastors by virtue of their office and the respect in which they are held in the community, have tremendous advantages when making calls. Pastors are the last professionals to make home visits, and seldom do they have a door slammed in their faces. And if they do, so what? They are then in good company, for Jesus was "despised and rejected of men" for their salvation.

I used to tell my students in the Juan Calvino Seminary in Mexico City that there were two pieces of leather they must expect to wear out if they wanted to plant churches and see them grow—the leather around their Bibles and on the soles of their shoes. One student took this advice seriously, and when he told me that the church to which he had been assigned over summer break had doubled in size, he added, "And maestro, I wore out three pairs of shoes!" He hardly needed to tell me, because churches seldom grow without a great deal of visitation. The concern the pastor shows in the time he spends calling becomes the model for the members of the congregation in their concern for one another and for outsiders. There is simply no substitute for the pastor's visits, in the home, the hospital, and wherever people are found.

Furthermore, it is excellent therapy for pastors to engage regularly in direct evangelism on strange and unfriendly turf. They need to face the same world ordinary church members confront day after day. Away from the security of the pulpit and church building pastors should expose themselves to hostile ridicule, barbed questions, and instant rejection. Jesus exposed Himself in that way, and we should not avoid it.

In the rough and tumble of the world the evangelizing pastor gains fresh insights into the non-Christian mind. When hecklers in a prison block, a campus gathering, or the open street challenge his religious assertions, he learns new things about human depravity and the harsh realities of evangelism. He finds what it takes to prepare and preach evangelistic messages without the use of familiar clichés and the religious background we tend to take for granted in the church. In my own ministry, some of the hardest messages I ever preached were in the open air before a mixed audience of Buddhists and Hindus, where anything, including violence, might be expected. And I never felt closer to the ministry of Jesus, who seldom enjoyed safe turf and was a street preacher who made

Himself vulnerable to hostile listeners.

More important than formal study is prayer. It takes a lot for a teacher of homiletics to say that, but I do. When the pastor has a passion for souls, it shines through in everything he does and says, especially his prayers in private and before the congregation. Parishioners who breathe an atmosphere charged by evangelistic passion conveyed through the pastor's sermons and prayers, and attested by his ministry among them and their neighbors, eventually partake of the same spirit. It grows on them, and they touch others. Their prayers echo his, and his ministry carries over into theirs. As Edgar Whitaker Work stated it, "The minister's own practice of prayer will have much to do with the evangelistic force of his sermons. If his sermon is based in prayer in the making of it, if he rises from his knees to go to the pulpit, a power goes with the sermon that opens the way to the hearts of men. Prayer as a background to preaching is a condition that we can little understand, and certainly cannot measure. Men of power in prayer cannot preach a sermon, no matter what the subject, without making it evangelistic."[4] Prayer makes the preacher, and prayer makes the pastor. Men of great prayer for the lost and straying turn churches into power-houses of evangelism.

Organizing the Church for Evangelism

Some pastors have special gifts in evangelism. Many do not. But all pastors have the responsibility to facilitate evangelism in and through their congregations. Pastoral leadership in evangelism extends from the pulpit and classroom to the people in the pew who are moved to action by the Word and the Spirit and encouraged by the pastor's interest and example. There is one step more, and it extends to the structures and programs of the church, including new ones created intentionally with outreach in mind.

In this area it is especially helpful to define clearly the target people. In one church I pastored we spelled out repeatedly to the congregation that in the geographical area around the church we

4. Work, pp. 41-43.

were aiming our evangelism program toward the "unsaved, unchurched, and uncared-for." There were plenty of people in all three categories. Some had a flimsy church connection but knew nothing of personal salvation through Christ. We worked through the Sunday school, youth organizations, and a chain of midweek evangelistic home Bible studies to reach them. Some of our neighbors had never been connected to any church. We found that a midweek women's program held at church and focused on fellowship and Bible study proved to be one of the most fruitful things we did to reach the unchurched. The physically and spiritually uncared-for were all around us, and the deacons were mobilized to respond to appeals for help, especially food, and to tie in their ministry with the overall evangelistic thrust of the church.

Physical and emotional needs are seldom found in isolation from spiritual needs, and evangelistic deacons are a church's vital link to a neighborhood where there are poor, troubled, and unsaved people. Pastors should have no fear of social ministries so long as they are not given a higher priority than the spiritual. In the past, mainline denominations went wrong at the point when social service was given a higher priority than evangelism. Churches stopped their former activities in evangelism and spiritual outreach and shifted to social service as their main concern. That shift precipitated the downward spiral of those churches and denominations.

In organizing a church for evangelism, therefore, the key factor is to work out what you believe to be the biblical priorities and then hang on to them tenaciously as you develop the program. The relation of the ministries of evangelism and social service is crucial, and in a biblically directed church it will not be a question of *either . . . or,* but of *both . . . and.* Evangelical churches can grow and keep growing when they emphasize soul-saving, life-transforming evangelism, and the promotion of justice and care of the poor. Priorities must be determined and maintained, but one without the other falls short of biblical principle and example. As Harvie M. Conn has forcefully pointed out, evangelism in the biblical sense means doing justice while at the same time preaching grace. Only then does the Holy Spirit—who in former ages moved the prophets in their ringing defense of the poor, and who shone through the healing, feeding ministry of Jesus and led the early church to establish diaconal ministries—communicate through the modern church the message of the forgiving and compassionate God.

A Pastor-Evangelist in Lima, Peru

Pastoring an evangelical church in the South American country of Peru can be a dangerous occupation. Violent attacks have been made in recent years against Protestant churches, and many pastors have been killed. In defense of their people, church leaders have dared to speak out against the terrorists, some of whom have direct government connections, and pastors live in daily fear of reprisals for their defense of the innocent. Evangelical churches have plunged into relief ministries, gathering food, money, medicine, and clothing for the hundreds of widows and orphans left as victims of the violence.

Pastor Pedro Arana leads a Presbyterian congregation in Lima, and he is actively involved in church planting in other areas. He is deeply committed to the organized church, pastoral care of the members, leadership development in the congregations, and vigorous evangelism of a kind that multiplies believers and churches. He blends ministry to the soul and body and trains his members in the same way. His letters are filled with evidence of pastoral ministry of the highest order, combining care and development of believers with evangelistic outreach and compassionate ministries among the poor. What follows is taken from one of Pastor Arana's recent letters:

> I have a pastoral purpose in mentioning the severe weather we have been having, because the weather has been affecting the shape of our ministry. Last week we received a visit from two ex-convicts asking help to buy medicine and clothing. Both were released from prison five months ago. They have no documents, house, job, nor any means to get work. One of them sleeps in abandoned cars, despite the cold weather. What, they asked us, could we offer them? Of course we offered the gospel of salvation. We also offered medical care. One of our deacons took them for a meal at a restaurant close to our church. I was reminded of the words, "You did it unto me." But

as time passes, a more striking verse is sinking in: "When you have done all that you were told, say, 'Useless servants are we, because we have only done that which we should have done.' "

A widow with three children, ages twelve, ten, and four, all of them injured in some way by the floods in the north, made contact with our church. They currently reside in a desert-like section of the city of Lima, without water, electricity or toilet. They live in a small room made of wood with a straw mat as their roof. This does not protect them from the nightly dew which in turn has caused the children to be sick for several weeks. We supplied them with food and blankets, but what they really need is a room made of durable materials to be built on donated land. The deacons of the church have taken action, and we are in the midst of carrying out plans.

In each of these cases the church has provided immediate solutions. But the most effective kind of relief, that of creating sources of employment, has been left uncompleted. We have not been able to take the next step toward development. The brethren who earlier accompanied me in both evangelism and social work now think that we should not take on more projects and programs. But it seems to me that social transformation will then remain only a dream.

There are basic needs that are growing in size and number each day, such as food, housing, clothing, health, education and jobs. I believe we should ask the Lord to stimulate our imagination in order to create new sources of work here in town and in the rural areas. It will be difficult, but not impossible. There are several brethren who are taxi drivers and mechanics, but unemployed. We could start with two projects, the first one being a taxi service. Other brethren in the interior of the country have farms producing coffee, cocoa and wood, and they are being exploited by the "middle men." If they had a truck, it would solve their problem. We have to organize the unemployed people or their needs will continue to go unmet.

Should I start this task? A work like this is a lot to handle for a local congregation. I find myself looking for God's direction just like I did in the early years of my ministry. How to carry out an urban pastoral ministry with so many spiritual, emotional, moral and material needs all around? How does one know how to start?

Pastor Arana has made many good starts, as the correspondence between us reveals. He preaches and teaches regularly in four locations, developing young congregations in each place. He is busy training elders and deacons for each church and is involved in numerous programs of his denomination. And he has put his life on the line by identifying with other pastors in their protest against violence from terrorist and government forces. He is, in short, a pastor-evangelist, declaring the Word of God, caring for believers, organizing the church for biblical ministries, and actively seeking the lost and wounded, bringing them home. In such people the Christian apostolate lives on.

The Contributors

Frank M. Barker, Jr. is pastor of the Briarwood Presbyterian Church, Birmingham, Alabama. After receiving a degree in Textile Engineering from Auburn University, he served in the United States Navy as a jet pilot for four years. Following his time in the military, he attended Columbia Seminary, where he received the Bachelor of Divinity and Master of Theology degrees. The Briarwood Presbyterian Church, which he pastors, is one of the leading congregations in the Presbyterian Church in America and is noted for its strong emphasis on personal evangelism, prayer, Christian discipleship, and world missions.

James C. Bland III is pastor of the Kendall Presbyterian Church, Miami, Florida. After graduating from the University of Maryland with a Bachelor of Science degree, he pursued graduate work at the same institution. He received his Master of Divinity degree from Gordon-Conwell Theological Seminary near Boston and a Doctor of Ministry degree from Westminster Theological Seminary in Philadelphia. For three years he served as Assistant Minister at the Coral Ridge Presbyterian Church in Fort Lauderdale, Florida. Before taking up his present pastorate in Miami, he served as Senior Minister of the First Presbyterian Church in Gadsden, Alabama. He is author of the book *Miracles and Their Spiritual Application* and contributing editor of *This Is the Life*.

Edmund P. Clowney is Associate Pastor of the Trinity Presbyterian Church in Charlottesville, Virginia, and Professor of Practical Theology, Emeritus, of Westminster Theological Seminary in Philadelphia. A graduate of Wheaton College, he earned his Bachelor of Divinity degree from Westminster Theological Seminary and a Master of Systematic Theology from Yale Divinity School, and he pursued graduate studies at Union Theological Seminary, New York. After ten years of pastoral ministries in Connecticut, Illinois, and New Jersey, he taught practical theology at Westminster Theological Seminary in Philadelphia for twenty-two years and served also as president of the seminary. Author of numerous books, essays, and journal articles, he has a worldwide reputation as a preacher and lecturer.

Roger S. Greenway is Executive Director of Christian Reformed World Ministries in Grand Rapids, Michigan. He spent four years as a missionary-pastor in Sri Lanka, followed by seven years as a church planter and seminary teacher in Mexico City. He served as the Latin America Secretary for the World Mission Board of the Christian Reformed Church for six years and later held a pastorate in Grand Rapids. Before assuming his present position, he was Professor of Missions and Gospel Communications at Westminster Seminary in Philadelphia. A graduate of Calvin College, he earned his Bachelor of Divinity and Master of Theology degrees at Calvin Theological Seminary and his Doctor of Theology at Southwestern Baptist Theological Seminary in Fort Worth, Texas. Author and editor of numerous books and articles in English and Spanish, he serves as editor of the missionary journal *Urban Mission*.

Terry L. Gyger currently serves as president of the School of American Church Planting, as well as Associate Pastor of Perimeter Presbyterian Church, Northwest Congregation, in Atlanta, Georgia. He holds the bachelor's and master's degrees from the University of Arizona and a Master of Divinity degree from Conservative Baptist Theological Seminary in Denver. He is founder and president of Men in Action, now known as Ministries in Action. He was the organizing pastor of Immanuel Presbyterian Church in Miami, Florida, and Coordinator of Church Development for the Mission to North America of the Presbyterian Church in America.

Dirk J. Hart is Minister of Evangelism for the Board of Home Missions of the Christian Reformed Church. He is a graduate of Calvin College, Westminster Theological Seminary in Philadelphia, and Calvin Theological Seminary in Grand Rapids. He pastored Christian Reformed churches in Nova Scotia, Quebec, and Ontario, Canada. As Minister of Evangelism for the denomination, he is responsible for helping churches meet the challenge of reaching their communities with the gospel.

Bartlett L. Hess is pastor of the Ward Presbyterian Church in Livonia, Michigan, a suburb of Detroit. A graduate of Park College, Missouri, he earned his Master and Doctor of Philosophy degrees at the University of Kansas, and a Bachelor of Divinity degree at McCormick Theological Seminary in Chicago. He began preaching at the age of nineteen, ministering to churches in Missouri and Kansas while in school. He pastored the Trinity Presbyterian Church of Chicago, the Warren Park Presbyterian Church of Cicero, Illinois, and the Ward Memorial Presbyterian Church in Detroit. In the course of his pastoral career he started two churches, the Trinity Presbyterian Church of Plymouth and Grace Chapel of Farmington Hills, Michigan. He plans to begin a new church this year in the Brighton area, outside Detroit. Ward Presbyterian Church, which he now pastors, has 4,500 members and continues to grow.

Richard P. Kaufmann is pastor of the New Life Presbyterian Church of Escondido, California. He teaches part-time at Westminster Theological Seminary in California in practical theology. He holds degrees from Bucknell University and the Harvard Business School and worked as a Certified Public Accountant for six years before entering Westminster Theological Seminary, Philadelphia, where he earned a Master of Divinity degree. The Kaufmann home is well known in the Escondido area as a center of love, hospitality, counseling, and discipleship.

D. James Kennedy is pastor of the Coral Ridge Presbyterian Church in Fort Lauderdale, Florida. He holds degrees from the University of Tampa, Columbia Theological Seminary, Chicago Graduate School of Theology, and Trinity Evangelical Divinity School, as well as a Doctor of Philosophy degree from New York University. He is the founder and president of Evangelism Explosion International, an interdenominational organization that trains ministers and lay persons to fulfill the Great Commission. This organization now works with over 200 denominations in sixty countries. The Coral Ridge Presbyterian Church has been the fastest growing Presbyterian church in the United States, growing in twenty-five years to over 6,500 members. Attendance at the four morning services exceeds 10,000, and the church is served by fourteen ministers. For the past sixteen years he has been a regular member of the faculty of the Billy Graham School of Evangelism and has lectured to over 75,000 ministers and seminary students. He is author of numerous books, including *Evangelism Explosion*, which has been translated into a dozen languages.

C. John Miller is pastor of New Life Presbyterian Church in Philadelphia. He taught evangelism at Westminster Theological Seminary for many years and is an associate evangelist for the Presbyterian Evangelistic Fellowship. He is the author of two books, *Repentance and Twentieth Century Man* and *Evangelism and Your Church*, and is working on a third, to be called *Outgrowing the Ingrown Church*. He is active as the senior pastor of one of the fastest growing churches in Philadelphia and in a number of home and foreign mission programs. With six other Presbyterian leaders he organized World Harvest Mission, a missionary-sending agency that works primarily in Uganda and focuses on church planting. He hopes to enlarge the program to reach Muslim countries.

T. M. Moore is the Executive Pastor of Ministries at the Church of the Saviour, Wayne, Pennsylvania, a suburb of Philadelphia. Until recently he served as Senior Vice-President of Evangelism Explosion III, International, in Fort Lauderdale, Florida. He is a graduate of the University of Missouri and Reformed Theological Seminary and is pursuing a doctoral degree at the University of Pretoria, South Africa. He has worked in the areas of campus ministry, Christian education, church planting, and executive management in a variety of ministry contexts. He is the author of four books and numerous articles dealing with church life and evangelism.

Harry L. Reeder III is the pastor of Christ Covenant Church in Charlotte, North Carolina. He previously served Presbyterian churches in Chattanooga, Tennessee, and Miami, Florida. A graduate of Covenant College at Lookout Mountain, Tennessee, he earned a Master of Divinity at Westminster Theological Seminary in Philadelphia and currently is pursuing a doctoral degree at Covenant Theological Seminary in Saint Louis, Missouri. He conducts a radio ministry called the "Christ Covenant Pulpit," which is heard daily on WHVN in Charlotte, North Carolina, and he is a frequent speaker in Bible and evangelistic conferences around the country.

Kennedy Smartt is the Coordinator of Evangelism for the Presbyterian Church in America with primary responsibility in the development and coordination of a multi-faceted plan of evangelism for the churches of the denomination. Prior to assuming this position he pastored churches in Scottdale, Georgia, and in Hopewell, Virginia. Following these pastorates, he served as Coordinator of Church Relations for Mission to the World, the foreign mission agency of the Presbyterian Church in America. He serves on the boards of Evangelism Explosion and *The Presbyterian Journal* and preaches at conferences and evangelistic meetings throughout North America.

Appreciation

I express the appreciation of all the contributors to Dr. Edna Greenway and Mrs. Sharon Fox for the many hours they spent preparing this book for publication.

The Editor